"How does a person continue on after experiencing numerous trials and sufferings in childhood and throughout life? Delaine's memoir of her life and her journey with God is an inspiring testimony of her amazing inner spirit. It also brings forth the role that family members play in being present to each other in a playful and joyful way in times of trials. Her story illuminates trust in God, leading her to a deep desire to live her best self, to help others to overcome their obstacles, to come out of the shadows, and to live in the Light."

— **Sister JoAnn**, Spiritual Director

"I think this book ought to be used by every mental health doctor, school counselor, and any other person who is working with others. I knew parts and pieces of your life, but not all put together so concisely as this is written and my thought is, 'Oh, this woman is strong physically, emotionally, and spiritually.' Not in the way of going out bench pressing, but in the way of dealing with all the tragic events of your life. "Your father and mother deserve a special place in heaven, the place where the folks go who carried the big crosses because both of them certainly had big ones to carry. I admire them for surviving the loss of Billy but not their marriage. That in and of itself says the kind of people they were."

— **Kay Langin**, Retired Senior Master Sergeant, US Air Force

"A smile. That moment when your lips part and the corners of your mouth inch toward the sky and a sense of joy enters your heart and warms the deepest parts. Even better are the laughs, the chuckles, and the giggles that often follow the cracking of a smile.

It's easy. Smiling is one of the simplest forms of human expression. Laughter is one of the most joyous. Yet, life often makes it hard for us to smile and to laugh. We all have the days when a health issue keeps us from living life to the fullest or the loss of a loved one makes you feel as if smiling is impossible. There are days when sorrow replaces happiness and tears stain our cheeks.

As I have worked with Delaine on her memoir, she has taught me that life is about finding laughter after moments that seem unbearable. It is not about letting the world break you, but instead letting it teach you to be the strongest version of yourself. She has taught me to never let life cripple your sense of humor, it is the best weapon you have in the fight for happiness."

— **Alexa Giebink**, author of "PHOENIX Rising from Addiction: Memoir of Mary Ann Giebink"

AND THEN, **WE** LAUGHED

AND THEN, **WE** LAUGHED

A Memoir

By Delaine Shay

XULON PRESS

Xulon Press
2301 Lucien Way #415
Maitland, FL 32751
407.339.4217
www.xulonpress.com

© 2018 by Delaine Shay

All rights reserved solely by the author. The author guarantees all contents are original and do not infringe upon the legal rights of any other person or work. No part of this book may be reproduced in any form without the permission of the author. The views expressed in this book are not necessarily those of the publisher.

Unless otherwise indicated, Scripture quotations taken from the Amplified Bible (AMP). Copyright © 1954, 1958, 1962, 1964, 1965, 1987 by The Lockman Foundation. Used by permission. All rights reserved.

Scripture quotations taken from the Holy Bible, New International Version (NIV). Copyright © 1973, 1978, 1984, 2011 by Biblica, Inc.™. Used by permission. All rights reserved.

Printed in the United States of America.

Cover designed by Nathan Shay

ISBN-13: 9781545639399

IN MEMORY OF MY PARENTS,
Jerry and DeVonna Weets

They taught and nurtured my faith in Jesus. The coping skills they developed going through hardships would play a vital role in how they lived out their married life. With all the pressure they were under, they also laughed. They laughed with their daughters, as well as friends and family as they gathered around our kitchen table.

When my parents celebrated their fiftieth wedding anniversary, the church party room was packed. Mom and Dad beamed and laughed as friends and relatives shared comical stories. Mom and Dad held hands. Mom even winked at Dad and said, "I got you Babe," referencing an old Sonny and Cher song. Dad winked back. I'm glad I saw it.

My folks made it through a lot of tragedies that would have split many marriages up. They did the best they could with love, discipline, caring, and humor.

ACKNOWLEDGMENTS

To my husband Owen: I could not have done this without you. You laughed with me and held me through my tears. You believed in me and encouraged me to keep writing. I love to hear you laugh and see you smile.

To all my grandchildren: Thanks for humoring me when I think I'm so funny and for putting up with my repeated stories about you. You all are a joy in my life!

To their parents, my stepchildren: Thanks for the great job raising your kids to be kind, respectful, responsible, able to laugh at themselves, and fun to be around.

Nathan Shay, what fun it was watching you as a young boy drawing, drawing and drawing. And *now*, as a professional creating the cover of my book.

OSL Writer's Group, I made it with your encouragement!

To Kay Langin, my pen pal exchanging a weekly letter for twenty-five years. During many rough health times, you were a connection for me and helped me know that I wasn't forgotten.

Thanks to Evelyn Leite for challenging me to grow and strive to be the best version of myself. You encouraged me and supported me to keep going through my past to gain healing.

Thanks to those who read my story, made corrections, asked questions, and encouraged me: Alexa Giebink, Brian Kaatz, Kay Langin, Sister JoAnn, Mary Ann and Brad Giebink, Adam Jerstad, Sunny Foster, June Witte, Margaret Novak and my sisters, Lucy Selland and Denita Dahl.

Alexa Giebink, thank you for your help in organizing, editing and prodding me along. You are not only brilliant, you are a compassionate, loving woman who helped me so much to bring this to fruition.

To Sharon Herrick McGilvrey, remember when we had to stay after school because we couldn't stop laughing in Mr. M's class? What a gift to have you in my life for over fifty years with lots of laughter.

Sally Swanson, thanks for being so darn honest with me and for your great laughter!

To Patty Meyers and Christina O'Hara, thanks for listening to me over and over as I strived to grow in faith. Your faith, love and laughter are such a godsend.

Every single person at every meeting I've ever gone to. Your stories told with such honesty and humility have helped me beyond measure. I'm grateful I am part of the first word, WE.

To all my dear family and friends for believing in me and loving me especially when I didn't love myself. There isn't enough paper to list all of your kindness and love.

Acknowledgments

To Pastors Julie Kahl, Paul Rohde, Nadine Lehr, Heidi Binstock, Tim Lemme, and Justin Kosec and many others; the Stephen Ministers who have walked and prayed with me in tears, laughter, healing and hope: Susan Wold Rohde, Inga Rohde, the late JoAnn Hanson, Connie Salmela and Janice Peterson.

Dr. Larry Keefauver for your wise words, "Surrender your expectations at the foot of the Cross and expect God." Sylvia Burleigh from Salem Publishing, thanks for your encouragement.

Foremost, to my Lord and Savior Jesus Christ. Thank You for putting the desire in me to tell some of my story and the healing and clarity I gained from it.

TABLE OF CONTENTS

Introduction: God's Timing xix

Chapter 1: Ready or Not; September 15, 1950 1
Chapter 2: Our Great Sadness; 1953 5
Chapter 3: Then Mom Left; July 1953 17
Chapter 4: A Child's Love; 1959 25
Chapter 5: A Summer Surprise; 1957 39
Chapter 6: Life as a Little Sister; 1959-1961 43
Chapter 7: Uncle Tommy; 1959-1960 53
Chapter 8: How to Get Help and How to Help; 1961 65
Chapter 9: I Just Wanted to Feel Good; 1964-1968 81
Chapter 10: Trying to Hang On; 1968 95
Chapter 11: The Fall; 1970 107
Chapter 12: It Is What It Is; 2010 141
Chapter 13: Happy Days; 1981 151
Chapter 14: A Smashing Beginning; 1983 167
Chapter 15: Out of Darkness; October 3, 1986 171

Chapter 16: Comic Relief; 1970 to the present........................183
Chapter 17: Healing by God, Through Time;
             December 1992..189
Chapter 18: When She Smiled; May 2007 201
Chapter 19: Faith..209
Chapter 20: Renewed Faith..221
Chapter 21: God's Timing to Tell the Story; 2004..................243

Conclusion...249
Epilogue: Gathering Pieces.......................................253
About the Author...257
Appendix: Serenity Prayer..259

"To boldly come out from hiding and offer our truest selves to the world; this is the work of the spiritual journey."

— Chris and Phileena Heuertz[1]

---

[1] www.sermoncentral.com/content/Chris-Heuertz

INTRODUCTION
GOD'S TIMING

The first time I saw psychologist Dr. Shelley in 1994, I told her about my brother Billy. I knew that after all these years there was still more for me to learn and understand about his death; something kept nagging at me to continue asking questions of the past. When a friend told me about some of the helpful therapy work she had done while seeing Dr. Shelly, I had a gut feeling that this therapist could help me continue to work out my childhood traumas.

When we met, I insisted on doing the exercise my friend had done. She created a life collage by placing photos and objects that represented her life onto a poster board. Dr. Shelly was surprised by my determination. After we'd had a few sessions, she told me I was the most pro-active client she had ever had. Maybe that was a nice way to say I was pushy. I was hungry for healing and determined to find answers. I needed to know what was eating me up inside.

I was forty-four years old when an abreaction occurred after several months in therapy. It was a beautiful spring day with the sun shining brightly into the office. My forest green wheelchair was parked behind the cozy armchair I was seated in.

For four years, I had been suffering with Chronic Fatigue and Immune Dysfunction that made my muscles often too weak to stand or walk except for short distances using crutches. The three lumbar back surgeries I had in my twenties and the one in my thirties compounded my weakness. I was so sure that I needed to visit the therapist that I asked a friend who worked near the doctor's office for help. Because I was frail, he lifted my wheelchair out of my car for me, and then he pushed me into the building and left me by the elevator. My teenage niece Valerie from Des Moines, Iowa was staying with us; I had her on my mind since she was back at the house alone.

I had barely settled into the session when it happened.

"Oh my gosh! I think I'm going crazy! I'm seeing something...oh my gosh! It's like a video playing!" I exclaimed.

"Stay with it if you can, you're okay," the doctor said. "I'm right here."

I didn't feel okay and I didn't know if I could go on. It was difficult to breathe as my chest tightened and my whole body was on high alert. I needed to get away, to run, but I did as she said and watched.

I saw myself as a little girl, moving and hearing things. This had never happened to me before. My memory had always been of me sitting still in the dirt, pouting because I'd been left behind.

I watched and listened as my two-year-ten-month-old body heard the screams and my Dad's voice shouting, "DON'T COME OVER HERE! DON'T COME OVER HERE! STAY THERE! NO, DON'T COME!"

I was standing. I turned to see Mom on the steps at the side door of our house facing toward the grain elevator across the street. Terror rose up in me as I saw a horrid look on her face.

As she started running to Dad, I cried for her to wait, "Mommy, Mommy!"

My little legs worked hard, pumping to try to catch her.

I kept crying for her, "Mommy! Mommy! Wait for me."

Quickly she turned and scooped up my little body. The screaming continued. I could also hear screaming from my two older sisters, Jerri and Lucy, and Uncle Tommy.

When we got to the elevator across the road from our house, I saw Billy in Dad's arms. He wasn't moving. My brother was so still. Mom reached for him as Jerri grabbed onto me. She held me tight as I fought, kicking and screaming, to get loose.

I watched as Mom and Dad, holding Billy, jumped into the back seat of a black car that sped away from us, kicking up dust.

As I sat in that chair shaking, the counselor assured me, "It's not happening now. Feel your feet on the floor. I'm right here with you. You're okay."

"That was a flashback," I said. "I remember reading about them in returning Vietnam soldiers."

As I was preparing to leave, I asked, "How am I going to be able to take care of my niece today?"

"Remind yourself of where you are, that the accident is not happening now," reassured the psychologist. "Some flashes may happen, but you can handle this, you aren't that child. Today was a breakthrough, you made good progress."

I left there shaken, but with some relief. The flashback that I somehow always knew was there had finally burst through.

"Jesus loves me this I know for the Bible tells me so. Little ones to Him belong, they are weak, but He is strong!"
— Lyrics from "Jesus Loves Me"

CHAPTER 1
READY OR NOT

SEPTEMBER 15, 1950

"You are **not** ready. I've had a baby myself, I know!" the nurse yelled angrily as my mom laid on the delivery table seething from pain.

She could not believe the nurse was refusing to call the doctor, and instead, was bossily yelling, "You're ready! I told you, now quit pushing!"

Trying to catch her breath between the contractions, Mom spit out, "Are you telling me you know my body better than I do? I have had three babies and I know this one is coming out **now**!"

No matter how passionately Mom begged the puffed-up nurse to call the doctor, she refused. While the two women argued, Dad was nervously standing outside the hospital smoking a cigarette. As he was pulling another drag, he heard Dr. Fisk's car drive up the dark rainy street. Dad was relieved to see the doctor's car pull into the hospital driveway and together, the two men hurried inside.

Dad was left in the waiting room as Dr. Fisk went to check on Mom. Dad burst through the door to see me, his new baby, nestled in Mom's arms. She was right. I took no time making my entrance into the world. Mom had her strong determination and faith to get her through. From the time of my birth, I was taught to be a fighter.

Named Delaine, after Mom's younger sister who had died of influenza when she was two years old, I was the fourth child. Jerrilyn had just turned four in June, five days earlier Lucy had her third birthday, and my only brother, Billy was sixteen months older than me. Baby of the family was my role for five years until my little sister, Denita was born.

On each birthday, Mom would tell me the story of my birth.

Every year, Dad would chime in, "You had so much hair you looked like a rat!"

Friends thought it was a terrible thing for a dad to say about his baby girl, but I always thought it was funny. He made me feel special with his smile and sparkling eyes.

"Trusting when our anguish has brought us to our knees, it has brought us into the position of prayer. Then we can be more fully open to God and our experience of pain will be transmitted from a soul toxic lead to the gold of compassion, gratitude and wisdom. This transformation gives us the ability to love and serve others more completely and in doing so redeems our suffering."

— Martha Beck[2]

---

[2] www.goodreads.com/author/quotes/12120.Martha._N_Beck

CHAPTER 2
OUR GREAT SADNESS

1953

It had happened in 1953, only two days before the big Fourth of July Celebration. Every year, Trent, South Dakota, hosted a parade that was only a few blocks from our house. There were floats, clowns, horseback riders, tractors, and fire engines flowing down the main street. On the grounds next to the spring-fed swimming pool, a carnival was set up complete with cotton candy, pony rides, a rodeo, a talent show, and fireworks at night. Excitement ran high! The little town of Trent was the place to be to celebrate our country's birth. For many years, all I knew about that day and the accident was what Mom later told me. I didn't know how to grieve or how to deal with my overwhelming feelings of loss and anger. So, I would act up out of frustration. As I grew older, many people told me to just get over it. They would dismiss me because they thought I was too young to even remember Billy. But I remember the great sadness that overcame me and the giant dark hole he left in my heart. Somewhere deep down in me a repressed memory had been begging to be let out.

After the flashback hit me, I found myself sitting in a chair in Dr. Shelly's office; I was shaking. The doctor told me I had an *abreaction* and gave me a sheet explaining it. What I experienced was a sudden release of a previously repressed emotion, attained through reliving the event that caused it.

I left the office shaken but with some relief. The flashback I always felt was there had finally appeared. I thanked God the revelation happened in a safe place where a professional could help me maneuver and understand what was happening to me.

Apparently, on Thursday, July 2, as I sat in the dirt outside our home, the kids took a detour on their way uptown to the grocery store. They crossed the gravel road from our house to say hello to our dad at the Quaker Oats Elevator. He was working that day driving a large grain truck. It had only been a couple of months since he had started with the company.

When I was in my fifties, I wanted to know more so I called Dad's old manager hoping to find out who took care of us kids when Mom, Dad, and Billy were whisked away, but he didn't know. When I heard him say that he had told Dad to keep us kids away from there, I cringed for my parents. That must have compounded the guilt they already felt. Talking to him gave me no relief, only more pain and shame.

In a newspaper clipping Mom kept, it was reported that Billy thought Dad was going to go forward so little Billy went behind the truck to help by pushing. Instead, Dad backed up.

The truck's large tire rolled over Billy's head, killing him instantly. I gasped when I read that the accident had been investigated and no charges would be brought against Dad. I'd never heard that had been a possibility.

My older sister Lucy wrote about it in a paper for her registered nursing degree: "Instead of going up town (to get the mail) though, we went over to the elevator where my Father worked. My Father was driving a large grain truck into the elevator. I remember swinging on the back end of it after it had stopped. My Father did not know we were there and started to back up. We all let go except for Billy. He hung on and fell. The truck ran over him."

Lucy continued that she didn't remember any more except for riding to the funeral in a big car. My oldest sister Jerri's memory was very clear, but I always thought it would hurt her too much to ask her about the accident, so I didn't. Now I can't as she died in 1997 of ovarian cancer.

At the local emergency room, the doctor took Billy's lifeless body from my parents' arms. He comforted them with the information that Billy died instantly. I think my parents knew as they rushed down the dirt road holding Billy in the back seat that he was dead, but who could blame them for holding out for a miracle.

The next time I saw Billy, he was lying in what looked like a box in our house. All I wanted was for him to get up and play with me! I wanted to hear his voice call me his pet name, Decer. I guess his little boy mouth couldn't say Delaine, so it came out as

Decer (Dee-sir). I didn't understand what was happening. Why wouldn't my parents and sisters stop crying and play with me?

Years later, I asked Mom why his casket had been in our house. It seemed gruesome to me. She said it was customary at that time to hold a funeral service in the home before the church service, but mostly she wanted her little boy home one more time. There was a regular funeral service at our home on Sunday afternoon with a pastor from the Trent Baptist Church (where Billy and my sisters went to Sunday school). A vocalist sang, "Jesus Loves Me" and "Tell Me the Story of Jesus".

Right afterwards, a funeral service was also held at my grandparent's Lutheran church in Flandreau. I don't remember being at the funeral; Mom was so emotionally devastated that she cannot recall if I was there or not, understandably.

She did tell me Dad cried as he stood by Billy's coffin saying to Mom he couldn't even pay for the funeral. I wonder if the shame of it all was beginning to add up and make him feel like less of a father. I hurt so much for my parents when Mom later told me about his hopelessness. Thankfully, his two older brothers pitched in and covered the costs of the funeral.

Recently, I was visiting with my older cousin, Sandy and she told me that her dad Rhine, Dad's older brother, got a call from my mom the day Billy died. After hearing there had been a terrible accident, Rhine left immediately to help his brother in any way he could.

Sandy explained to me, "My dad would really watch out for your dad over the years. He (Dad) would come to our house for coffee at least once or twice a week."

Blessedly, Dad had a flexible job selling feed and fertilizer to farmers that enabled him to spend much needed time with his older brother as well as visiting his other siblings who lived close.

When I was an adult, Mom told me that some people who came to the house days before and after the funeral would take Billy's toy truck off the piano and put it out of sight. I suppose they thought seeing it would remind Mom of all she had lost, but Mom said she would always find where they hid it and put it right back on the piano.

It was a precious reminder of her little boy and the fun he had playing with it. Even though it brought her sorrow, it also brought a smile to her heart when she recalled the good memories of how happy he had been playing with it. Mom told me that once I conked Billy on the head with the truck, but instead of getting mad, he sweetly said, "Don't, Decer."

Billy was my best friend. He was a kind older brother and a fun pal to get in trouble with. When he died, Billy was nearly bald. Several weeks before, Billy and I were with Mom at a store in a nearby town. While she was busy shopping, we grabbed a pair of scissors and playfully cut each other's hair. It was so bad that Dad had to take us to the barber where Billy got a near buzz cut and my choppy locks were evened out.

In the days following Billy's death, I would hear many people comment, "Oh, how sad. He was their only boy."

For years, I felt it would have been easier for my parents if I had been the one to die instead. As I grew older, it seemed to me they could have spared one daughter out of the four, but not their only son. This little kid thinking subconsciously tormented me for years as I thought my life was not as valuable as other people's.

I didn't realize or understand until much later in life that I had always tried to make up for Billy's death to my parents. In an attempt to comfort Mom and Dad, I worked extra hard to make them proud of me. I was naturally scrappy, so I did my best to fill the role of a son, especially through sports such as swimming and softball.

In the family, only Billy and I had blonde hair and green eyes. Sometimes Mom would brush my hair back and say reminiscently, "You look just like Billy." When he died, I was the blonde sheep in a family of brown haired beauties.

Several times, when my sisters and I were with Mom shopping, adults thought it was cute to ask me if I was adopted. The image of me standing next to my lovely sisters with their rich brown hair and deep brown eyes brought to life the feeling that I didn't belong. I desperately wanted to look like my sisters, thinking that would make me a legitimate part of the family. I was just as much a loved part of the family as anyone else, but reason is seldom found when a child goes through a trauma.

When I would ask Mom if I was adopted, she would kindly remind me, "No, remember Billy had blonde hair and green eyes, too."

We had received our green eye color from Mom and my heart always warmed when I would see her green eyes gazing lovingly at me.

Those negative thoughts and encounters rubbed hard against the wound of Billy's death. Each reference to my being different served as a cold reminder that my Billy was gone. Without him, I yearned unproductively to fit in somewhere.

Eventually, I learned that this gnawing loneliness was part of survivor's guilt. This guilt would play a big role in the choices I made later in my life. A decade later, my first drink of alcohol that burned its way down my throat was an attempt to drown my guilt and shove it down so far that I would never have to deal with it in the cold light of day again. I talked with Mom and a number of ministers about it, then began going to counseling at age nineteen in the midst of a nervous breakdown—that's what they called it back then. Twenty some years later, I finally had a breakthrough.

Some families back then had a habit of not talking with each other about serious topics, but my Mom was always open to talk with my sisters and me about Billy and about God. She said that Grandpa and Grandma Weets would study the Bible with her and Dad after the accident. I think that it helped her deal with her emotions and allowed me to battle my grief. By reminiscing about Billy's and my shenanigans, we kept his gleeful spirit alive.

Mom kept an eight by ten framed photo of Billy on top of the china cabinet next to our front door. Mom had his shoes bronzed and they were displayed inside the cabinet next to a little blue rocking horse they received as a gift when Billy was born.

The big Trent Celebration on July 4, 1953 went on as planned. Mom told me that some of the organizers came to the house to apologize and to tell Mom and Dad that they felt terrible, but there was no way to contact all the participants to cancel.

At the same time, Mom somewhat cut us girls off from Dad. I suppose she wanted to protect him from the pain of our questions. I remember her saying, "Don't upset your dad."

My sister Lucy described it well, "We were always walking around on eggshells."

I certainly understand why Mom did that. She kept us moving forward. She was the rock of our family.

After Billy's death, our family received money from friends and family for memorials. My parents used some of it to buy pictures of the Lord's Supper to hang in both the Trent Baptist Church and Bethania Lutheran church in the country that we later joined. The picture from the Baptist Church now hangs in our home office.

Mom decided that some of the memorial money would be spent on a television set. That might sound odd or offensive to those who gave memorials, but she knew our family desperately needed some entertainment, a distraction from the pain threatening to cripple us all. So, we plugged into the sitcom of the day and then we laughed.

Childhood Memories

I was two years and ten months old when he died. Some family and friends have questioned whether I could really remember, but the flashback in Dr. Shelly's office definitely revealed more to me and I consider it as one of God's awesome gifts.

Over the years, I've often asked others what their first childhood memories were and how old they were. It greatly soothed and strengthened me when a dear friend, Alma, told me when she was three years old she remembered seeing her mom dressed in a long red coat throwing a snowball at her dad.

I have paid close attention to kids at that age and now especially our grandchildren. I have watched to see just how much they remembered about relationships and how they interacted with their siblings and others. I saw them being very relational and acutely aware of parting from each other. One of our grandsons shed alligator tears whenever it was time for us or them to leave. Seeing this, I came to more fully trust the relationship I had with Billy—what I remembered and what was revealed to me.

For years my only recollection of that day was a photo in my mind of me sitting in front of the house playing in the dirt, feeling lonely. These feelings of pain and abandonment are threads that have woven through the rest of my life.

I have also learned that you don't get over the loss of a loved one, you have to learn to live over it. It took a lot of work and God's grace to do that and it required the help of others—counselors, pastors, family, friends, and my spiritual mother, Sister

DelRey, who let me lay my head in her lap and sob the tears I wasn't able to cry with Mom.

I can still feel DelRey's hands running over my forehead and hair, her voice soothingly and gently saying, "Cry. Make the sounds. The grief has been in there a long time. Go ahead and cry."

It has continued to amaze me that Mom and Dad made sure that every July 4th Celebration in Trent was a fun time for us. Lots of family including grandparents, aunts, uncles and cousins, would gather at our place for a pot luck and then go on to the festivities. One year my cousin Mike even got a fire truck to make a call to our house when he threw a cherry bomb in some weeds across the street from our house. Every year Mom made sure that we girls had new shorts outfits.

It wasn't until I was much older that I realized what Mom and Dad had been going through to see us happy. Their strength to do that had to come from God and His mighty grace. I wish I could tell them right now how very much I admire their faith and love.

I'm not sure what year I started doing it, but I would call them in the morning of every May 12, Billy's birthday. We didn't say much, but we were bonded beyond words. I did it for me as much as for them. It was God working His healing power in and through me.

"There is in every true woman's heart, a spark of heavenly fire, which lies dormant in the broad daylight of prosperity, but which kindles up and beams and blazes in the dark hour of adversity."

— Washington Irving[3]

---

[3] https://www.brainyquote.com/topics/adversity

CHAPTER 3
THEN MOM LEFT

AUGUST 1953

A few weeks later, a tumor was found on Mom's ovary. She knew something didn't feel quite right, so she went to the doctor in Dell Rapids, the same doctor who had pronounced Billy dead just weeks before. She was admitted to the hospital and a surgery revealed a grapefruit size tumor.

I felt so scared, with more fear piling on my already worried self. To me, it was as if Mom had died too. I was never allowed to visit her in the hospital and I couldn't understand where she had gone; I was full of fear that I'd never see her again.

Since Dad had not been working at the grain elevator for long, Mom was not covered by medical insurance. She pleaded with the doctor to wait just a few weeks to do the surgery, so she could have health insurance, but he felt it was imperative to operate immediately.

The doctor removed the tumor as well as her fallopian tube and ovary on one side of her body. During the surgery and hospitalization, my sisters stayed with our aunt and uncle, while I was sent to stay with Grandma and Grandpa Joe and my nine-year-old Uncle Tommy in Flandreau, SD. Regardless of the circumstances, I felt they had all abandoned me just like Billy had.

Children were not allowed to visit in the hospital, so for two weeks I craved Mom's presence, but it was denied. The separation felt like forever. Of course, she missed my sisters and me as much as we missed her.

In my twenties, Mom told me she was eaten up with worry about all of us as she laid in the hospital bed, but especially about Dad. Their mutual suffering created an urgency to be with each other, to mourn and heal together. They desperately needed each other to survive the tough times. Growing up, I had never paid attention to how deep their love and devotion to each other went. I wish I could tell them now how much I admire them and what good examples they were for sticking together.

I'm sure my parents held their breaths for weeks before getting the results of the biopsy. Then they were told by the doctor it was benign. God's presence was surely felt when they received the good news. What a relief that our family didn't have to cope with cancer so soon after Billy's death. The removal of Mom's fallopian tube and ovary on one side of her body lessened her chances of getting pregnant again, but miraculously my sister, Denita, nicknamed Nina, was born two years later.

The saying "adversity makes one strong" is true. Mom was formidable right up until she passed away of heart failure at the age of eighty-six. Like me, she was faced with pain and the need to persevere at a young age. Her grandparents had immigrated from Norway. She was the oldest of five children. When Mom was four, her two-and-a-half-year-old sister, Delaine, died of influenza while being held in her mom's arms. As a preteen, she had to take care of her mother and sister who suffered from Rheumatic Fever while her dad was working. When she was sixteen, her dad wanted her to quit school to take care of the family, but she stood her ground and achieved her high school diploma, going on to earn her teaching certificate.

As an adolescent, Mom battled arthritis while trying to keep up with her school friends. At nineteen, she looked her best friend's murderer in the eye as she testified against him during the trial. Her friend's fiancé had become so jealous when he saw her talking to another man, he strangled her and dumped her body in the stock tank located on her parent's farm. Earlier that day, Mom had seen the couple exiting a movie theater. Her testimony helped send him to the federal penitentiary for life.

At twenty-three, she eagerly accepted the marriage proposal of her sweetheart when he asked her to be the mother of his children. She ignored the comments of concern that he was four years younger than her and a German.

She was only thirty-two when she heard the screams at the nearby grain elevator and held her son's lifeless body in her arms as they rushed to the hospital. Mom stood strong for Dad and the rest of the family when we couldn't bear the weight of the tragedy ourselves.

Tragedies continued to pelt Mom right up to her death. She outlived many beloved family members including: her son Billy; her brother Tommy; three sisters: Delaine, Beverly and Jackie; her daughter Jerri, her husband Jerry and a son-in-law Steve Selland

Eventually, Mom's body began to shake from the stress. A lifetime of tragedy was finally adding up and she confessed she couldn't bear to talk about Billy anymore. The pain had filled her up, but even in her brokenness, she was a source of strength and joy for many, including myself.

Her whole life Mom was cheerful and young at heart. I credit her ability to weather the storms of life to these characteristics. As far back as I can remember, Mom could be mischievous, catching us off guard with her pranks. One day when I was eleven, I was at the kitchen sink helping Mom do the dishes. She was drinking a glass of ice water to cool herself from the hot summer sun shining in the window. Suddenly, she turned to me and tossed the remaining water drops into my face! Her laugh was so infectious that I couldn't help but laugh along with her. It didn't matter what hardship my family was fighting our way through, she always tried to infuse a little fun in our lives.

Nina, then five years old, saw Mom's horseplay that afternoon and thought it was funny. Later that evening, when I was lying in bed, she burst into the room and doused me with a full glass of water! My bed and I were soaked. However, this time I did not find it funny. I had a hot temper like Dad, so I immediately sprang out of bed and angrily chased after her. I wanted to make her pay, but Dad intervened. Although Mom would still catch one of us with a splash of water, Nina never again gave me a bedtime bath!

Mom was always surprising me with mischiefs and pranks. When I was thirteen, Jerri and Lucy had a dance party in our newly built detached garage. Graciously, they let me join in on a few of the dances I had often practiced with them in our living room. For the music, their friends brought seven-inch 45 rpm records to play on our Hi-Fi stereo. After the party, Jerri's friend Ginger spent the night. The next morning, when she was ready to go home, her Elvis Presley record *Rocka-Hula Baby* was nowhere to be found. Several weeks later, I came across it stashed in a cupboard above the refrigerator.

When I showed it to Mom, she got the funniest look on her face and said, "I really like it. When you girls go to school, I put it on and dance!"

Mom's strong presence in my life is a primary reason I did not fall even farther when I tumbled out of control in my young adult years. She was both a role model and a solid support in life even though I was rebellious and at the time didn't think adults or anyone in power knew what they were doing.

As I have gotten older, I have learned to follow Mom's lead when it comes to persevering through the tough times and indulging in a laugh whenever there's an opportunity. However, it took me a long time to live my life in such a way. I muddled my way through many years of anger, self-doubt, self-pity, and grief. Mom did, too. I certainly don't want to portray her as a saint because she had her faults. After Billy's accident, she fearfully clung to me. She would talk about her life's sorrows with me and we became enmeshed, though it wasn't healthy for either of us.

When Mom was moved to the nursing home, she told me she was afraid to tell others her life story because she feared they would think she made it all up. She thought others would write her off as an attention seeker who exaggerated events in her past. I believe Mom would approve of sharing our stories. This book is also a way for Mom to be heard and for her strength and courage to inspire others.

In a recent conversation, my cousin Sandy told me that her mother, Dad's sister-in-law, called Mom the rock of our family.

Warmly I replied, "Mom would have loved to hear that."

Friendship *is a gift that is fair in all things. It roots from one's heart and involves memories that stay not for a while but for a lifetime.*

— Unknown[4]

---

[4] http://www.searchquotes.com/search/Childhood_Friends_Memories/#ixzz581fW96YZ

CHAPTER 4
A CHILD'S LOVE

1959

The Olson family lived down the gravel road from us in Trent. They were a colorful group who played a large part in many of my early childhood memories. They offered comfort and comic relief to my family in our time of need after Billy's death. Even today, I let out a laugh as I remember all the shenanigans I got into with their son Kenny.

Kenny's dad, Gordy, had a hearty laugh and a quick temper like my Dad. His mom, Dorothy, was fun with a great sense of humor and a big heart. Kenny's oldest sister, Nancy, was best friends and partners in crime with my sister Lucy. We both had several more sisters who added to the jovial chaos. My youngest sister Nina was sandwiched between Kenny's sisters Peggy and Patty. Jerri was my oldest sibling and Julie was their youngest. We had fun together and we loved each other.

Kenny, born in 1949, was just a few months younger than my brother Billy. He loved calling me Decer, the precious nickname Billy gave me. Looking back, I can see what a blessing it was that I inherited Kenny after Billy's death.

As little kids, it didn't matter that Kenny was a year older than me. We loved having our September birthdays a day apart. We became fast friends. At that age, we didn't have the ability or understanding to know how much we loved each other or even have the maturity to understand what love was. I think I grew attached to Kenny because of the hole Billy left in my heart.

Kenny and I would run all around town barefoot, collecting pop bottles to redeem for a penny, getting into trouble and giving our parents gray hair. If there was a mud puddle to jump in, we'd hold hands and go for it. Any tree was game for us to climb or at least try. We did everything together—rode bikes, built forts, and even stole cigarettes from our parents. At the time, we conveniently thought of it as just borrowing them.

One day when we were hiding in our tree fort surrounded by weeds, our Gestapo sisters, Lucy and Nancy, caught us with the cigarettes and instantly ran to tell our moms.

After I was dragged home, my mom sat me down at our kitchen table, slapped a pack of cigarettes on the table and said, "Here's what you wanted. Now smoke 'em!"

Here was my big chance, but suddenly the thrill of smoking had been replaced with fear. I didn't even raise my hand to touch them.

Kenny's family had a wonderful house that to me was like a mansion with two staircases. The one off the kitchen was narrow and it felt secretive while the other was a beautiful wood staircase in their living room.

When I was about three years old, I got my head stuck between two of the ornate posts that were midway up the elegant oak front staircase. I can still hear my panicked screams and see Kenny, along with a mob of our sisters, frantically running to get our mothers. My mom and Dorothy pondered over what to do. How were they going to get me out?

Finally, Dorothy said, "Well, we may have to just saw it off."

Immediately, all the kids cried and begged, "Don't cut if off! Don't cut it off!"

Of course, Mom and Dorothy were talking about sawing a post off, not my head as the kids feared. Our mothers shared many a hearty laugh when recalling my stunt. It's fun to think back on our childhood adventures like this one and smile. I share these stories with my grandchildren, once again laughing about my comical past.

One day, Kenny and I broke into my Uncle Elmer's house. We knew he and Aunt Bessie were vacationing in California. That morning we didn't wake up intending to break into anyone's house. We were just playing an innocent game of throwing rocks at the house. Unfortunately, we took our boredom out in some naughty ways. All of a sudden, a rock hit the glass and crash went a window!

Since the window was now open, sort of, we decided to go in and look around. Our childhood curiosity could not resist climbing through the window to see what was on the other side. Kenny and I were both too short to get high enough to swing ourselves through the window, so our neighbor, Cynthia boosted us up and we crawled inside. We knew she didn't want to get in trouble, but we ordered her to help. As soon as we were inside, she quickly ran to tell my mom what we did.

I felt bad as Mom walked around the house asking, "How am I going to tell my uncle what you did? He asked me to watch his place while they were gone. How am I ever going to tell him what you did?"

The worst part was waiting for Dad to get home and finding out how naughty I had been.

His usual words were, "What in the hell is wrong with you? Do you have shit for brains?"

Well, I heard it enough and came to believe that I did. Later in life, I found out that some of my cousins heard that admonition from their dad, too.

What a whooping I got that night! Needing a pillow to sit on was becoming much too familiar to me, but that didn't end our shenanigans.

Sometimes Kenny and I had help getting into mischief. Our adventures were occasionally initiated and exacerbated by our sisters Lucy and Nancy. Because they both thought Kenny and I were so cute together, they decided one day we should kiss. Being as scrappy as I was back then, instead of kissing Kenny, I bit his thumb hard. I didn't like seeing him cry, but I was not going to kiss him!

One summer day, Lucy and Nancy locked Kenny and me in an old chicken coop behind our house. Immediately, I started to panic. I needed out now! No matter how much I begged and cried, they would not open the door.

If they weren't going to let us out, I was going to get us out myself! So, I reared back with my thin six-year-old body and kicked out the back window with my left leg. I had on shorts, so the breaking glass produced a huge V-shaped gash just below my knee. Our sisters got that door opened fast! Then with blood gushing down my leg and tears pouring down my cheeks, I hobbled to the house crying for Mom.

Lucy kept begging me, "Don't tell Mom, please don't tell Mom."

Based on the size of my inverted V scar, I should have been taken to the doctor to have it stitched up. Later they told me that we didn't have the money. Over the years, I've gotten a lot of storytelling mileage out of the large scar that resulted from my injury. I especially enjoy telling the story when Lucy is around.

Potentially the most unsafe, yet most exciting stunt we ever pulled occurred when I was about nine. A new three-story elevator building was being erected where Dad worked. Lucy, Nancy, Kenny, and I would sneak over to play on the wood frames. We would take turns using a pulley operated platform to pull each other to the top. My stomach squirms looking back on our stunt since now I am terrified of heights.

Another dangerous situation started with a desire to roast marshmallows. Kenny's mom was gone for the day, so he and I kept ourselves occupied by raking leaves in their backyard. When we had gathered up a huge pile of leaves, we found some matches and lit it up!

The flames burned high as Kenny and I stood back and admired our work ready to get the marshmallows going. It was a pleasant time until the field next to Kenny's house started on fire!

"Oh boy, we're really in trouble now!" I yelled as we ran for help.

When we saw the field catch fire, we knew exactly where to go and what to do because during one of our previous exploits, we had snooped through the unlocked volunteer fire department station. Together, Kenny and I dashed across lawns and shot over the railroad tracks. We panted as we continued to run past the white stucco post office, the old hardware store, the corner gas station, and finally reached the fire station.

Tearing open the door, we turned to the left and pulled the siren on. We held our aching sides as we gasped for breath and waited for the first volunteer to show up so we could tell him where the fire was. Then, we ran as fast as we could back to Kenny's house to try to do some damage control. By then nearly everyone in our small town of 200 people had already seen the smoke. The fire truck arrived before us and extinguished the fire promptly. The only thing left burning when the excitement was over was the fire on our backsides from the spankings we got.

A Child's Love

The following spring, the smell of smoke woke my mom in the middle of the night. Sometime previously, a fuse had blown. Because we didn't have a new fuse, Dad took the blown fuse out, put a penny behind it and then put the fuse back in to complete the electrical connection. This was a common practice back then.

However, the need to put in a new fuse was forgotten. The circuit was overloaded, and the fuse box located next to Nina's and my bedroom started on fire.

Quickly, Mom roused Dad to get us kids out of the house. He yelled for Jerri and Lucy to get up and get out. The fire was raging in my bedroom. As Dad carried us out of the house with one girl tucked in each arm, the ceiling collapsed in a heap of flames onto our bed. Meanwhile, Mom's bare feet pounded the gravel road, racing to the fire station. She told me with each breath she prayed for us to make it out safely, but she also feared the worst.

A few days later after things had calmed down a bit, Mom told me she was relieved she knew where to go and what to do as she ran for help. If Kenny and I hadn't set fire to a field, she would not have known what to do. This is only one example of how God took something bad and used it for good—used it to save my family's life.

As soon as Dad got us outside the burning house, Lucy assured me, "Dee, don't worry, I got your silver dollars!"

At the time, I admired her for rescuing my little treasure. Our lives were at stake, but Lucy made sure to grab the silver dollars! Over the years, we have had many good laughs about that. I still have those silver dollars, a reminder of our trials and tribulations.

After escaping, Lucy and I watched our home burn from the window of Kenny's bedroom. Jerri and Nina went to stay with other friends. As a third grader, I couldn't grasp the significance of it all, but was thrilled by the excitement.

I can't begin to imagine what my parents felt as they watched their home engulfed in flames. Of course, they were grateful we had all gotten out safely but Mom carried a heavier burden. She stood there full of fear knowing that she had not paid our house insurance premium that month.

As soon as she could, Mom called the insurance agent who lived twenty miles away. Through tears, she explained the house fire and her failure to pay the bill. Graciously, he said if she got the money to him that day, he would make sure it was covered. It was a good lesson for us kids in how kind and forgiving people can be, plus how Mom's humility and courage helped us. Throughout our young adult years when we owned our own homes, Mom harped at us to make sure our insurance premiums were paid. She was never again late.

After the fire, we had some good fortune. Dad worked with a man who had just bought a house not far from ours. His family wouldn't be moving in for several months and he welcomed us to stay there. It was a roof over our heads, but I didn't like it. It was dark and it wasn't home. I felt displaced.

The day we moved back home was a happy day for me and a stressful one for my parents. Dad couldn't find someone to fill in for him at work so Mom, my two older sisters, and I moved us back into our house. I mainly watched Nina who ended up getting the measles that morning.

If someone would have said to my folks, "God won't give you more than you can handle," they would have been punched in the nose.

Of course, we believed that God was helping us, but it doesn't mean we were not overwhelmed.

Dad was a self-taught carpenter, so he did most of the remodeling to our house. Thankfully, we had the insurance money. My sisters and I worked after school prying up the tiles on the kitchen floor. I might not have been much help, but I felt important being a part of the remodeling.

Dad used this opportunity to modernize our home with an indoor shower and bathroom. Up until that time, we used a slop pail inside a wooden frame Dad had built. Going to the bathroom indoors on an ivory throne was the silver lining of our house fire. Before the fire, we took baths in a square tub of water Mom would fill for us. I surely appreciated the modern comforts. Being hospitable, I invited the neighbor kids to enjoy the new shower that Dad installed.

A couple years before the fire, Kenny's first day of first grade came and I was devastated. Mom watched as I walked with Kenny across the street and through the park until we reached the gravel road that led to the elevator. Here we stopped because Mom said I could not go any further. Innocently, Kenny and I kissed each other goodbye. Tears rolled down my face as I watched him, his sister, my two sisters, and our neighbor cross the road and continue the six blocks to school.

Again, I was alone in the dirt with my heart crushed. I realize now that Kenny leaving me behind touched on the deep wound of losing Billy. Some of the adults in the town learned about the kiss and would tease us. To them our love was cute and insignificant, but to us it was sacred. It was an innocent love only children are capable of. No one realized how much we helped each other survive.

The years continued to bring sorrow. Our house fire was in April of 1959, Grandpa Weets (paternal) died of colon cancer on my ninth birthday in September of 1959, and Grandma Weets died of stomach cancer six months later. The next year in November, my uncle died.

Everywhere around me people were dying, and I did not understand why. Several weeks later, Dad had the first of his nervous breakdowns and was hospitalized for a number of weeks. I tried hard to hide my sadness and fear, but seeds of depression that had been planted inside me long ago continued to grow. It was too much.

Around the same time, Kenny and his family moved to Ventura, California. It was heartbreaking for both of us as the Olson family piled into their black car and drove away. I couldn't breathe; it was all too much. Why was I left behind in the dirt crying again? Kenny and I promised we would not forget about each other.

The family left their little black dog Curly with us who I could hug when I was crying and missing Kenny. My parents were far from thrilled when they learned she was going to have puppies, but I was ecstatic.

Several months after Kenny moved, the black dial phone with a long curly cord attached to our kitchen wall rang. It was for me! It was my first ever phone call and it was Kenny! During the following days, I told anyone and everyone about that call. I have never forgotten that thrilling feeling.

Kenny leaving for school and then moving to California was very traumatic for me. I felt like I had lost part of myself. And I had. Again, the wound left by Billy's death was reopened and it would take decades to heal.

After the phone call, Kenny sent me a letter with a picture of him and his dad in California. Inside was an ink pen and bracelet that I treasured. But gradually our relationship faded—it was too expensive to make phone calls. Once or twice Lucy and I would sneak into the kitchen and called the Olson's. Quickly, we were caught.

Several years later, in 1963, Kenny and his family moved back to Trent. They arrived in a large camper that to small town me seemed very glamorous. But it wasn't the same as before. I was intimidated by this big city boy who had lived all the way across the country.

He had dwelled in the exotic, magical state of California while I remained in our dinky South Dakota town. My best friend turning into a stranger compounded the feeling of not knowing who I was, a feeling that lasted for many years. Later, we both went to the same high school, but we had different interests.

Several years ago, my phone rang. When I answered, I heard the familiar nickname "Decer" and I knew exactly who was calling. It was strange hearing someone besides my family using that old and hallowed nickname.

After talking for a while and getting caught up he said, "I should have married you."

I broke into laughter and said, "Oh, Kenny, I was no prize."

Today, we rarely see each other, but the tender love we had remains. The love of sharing each other's early lives and being there for each other in the loss of Billy united us. Those memories can still touch on that tender wound of losing Billy, but now I know how to deal with those emotions.

I truly believe that God gifted me with Kenny when I needed him the most.

When the Olson family moved to California, it was one of the hardest times of my childhood. Our mothers would laugh at the kitchen table; Kenny and I would laugh as we jumped in mud puddles outside. Life may have taken the Olson family away, but it could never take away the fond memories of the time we shared.

"But when one does not complain, and when one wants to master oneself with a tyrant's grip—one's faculties rise in revolt—and one pays for outward calm with an almost unbearable inner struggle."

— Charlotte Brontë[5]

---

[5]   http://www.searchquotes.com

CHAPTER 5
A SUMMER SURPRISE

1957

In the summertime, Mom and Dad made sure that we girls knew how to swim and that we often got to go swimming in the wonderful spring-fed pond not far from where we lived. The Town Board hired a full-time lifeguard; some male citizens men in town built a tall wooden stand for the beach plus boy's and girl's changing room made of cinder blocks. As a teen it was my sister Lucy and my job to clean those and pick up garbage on the beach. The townsmen also built a dock, a tower placed in the deepest waters complete with high and low diving boards and a raft. It wasn't uncommon for a turtle or small snake to make an appearance. When my sisters and I were younger, Mom would sit on a bench near the concession stand watching us and visiting with other mothers.

During the summer of 1957, while I was toweling off in the bathhouse, Mom came in and noticed two lumps on either side of my pubic bone. I was a thin little thing, so the golf ball sized protrusions really alarmed her.

Mom hurried outside to ask her friend, who happened to be our county health nurse, to come in and to see what the lumps were. The whole ordeal embarrassed me, but I didn't have a choice. I had to do what I was told and let the lady look. Unsettled by what she saw, she urged Mom to take me to the doctor.

At his office, it was confirmed that the two bulges were hernias, which were unusual for someone almost seven years old. With this diagnosis, I was scheduled for surgery at the Dell Rapids Hospital. Hernias are genetic often skipping generations. My (maternal) Grandpa Joe also had a double hernia.

I was nervous the day of the surgery. The hospital room felt unwelcoming with curtains separating two beds with stiff looking sheets. My young brain didn't understand what was going to happen.

Right before surgery, the doctor came in the room with a friendly smile. I laid on the bed quietly, wanting to be good. I was relieved that Mom and Dad were there. With a warm smile, he bent down, picked me up, and carried me to the operating room.

Although I didn't know it at the time, he was the same doctor that over four years before had held my brother Billy in his arms and pronounced him dead. On the operating table, a mask for ether was put over my face and a dreadful, horrendous spinning ensued. Around and around my head spun until I fell unconscious.

A Summer Surprise

When the surgery ended, I woke up sick and threw up. The doctor entered my room to report to my parents the success of the procedure. After the horrible spinning of the ether, I no longer found his smile friendly. In fact, I did not like him and didn't want him in my room because I didn't know if he had something more planned. Thankfully, he said the surgery went well and I would be able to go home soon. It was a great relief that during my recovery, my sister Jerri stayed with me and shared my bed. I was so glad to have her there; she was a natural care giver.

As I settled into my bed at home, I was grateful the surgery was over and hoped I would never have to go through pain like that again. Little did I know that my double hernia surgery at seven years old was only the first of many health problems that continue to this day.

I usually had the support of family and friends when another ailment arose, but I often felt alone. When I was little and my feelings were hurt, I would crawl under our dining room table to sit alone and lick my wounds, all the while hoping someone would coax me out and hold me.

My self-defense mechanism was often to isolate myself, even though I really wanted to be with someone.

When life feels as if it is too much to bear, I try to take a step back and appreciate the little moments with loved ones. They are the real treasures in life.

CHAPTER 6
LIFE AS A LITTLE SISTER

1959-1961

Family has always been important to me. Growing up, we went through a myriad of things together—good and bad. Some lights in the darkness of my life have been my sisters. Often, they were there for me when I needed them. We have had our tiffs, but we always come back to a place of love.

Our histories are rich with stories of sticking together.

Jerri, four years older than I, impressed me with her faith. As a young girl, she prayed devoutly. I would see her lying on her bed loyally reading Evangelist Billy Graham's *Devotion Magazine*.

In the fall of 1996, she called me from her home in Charlotte, North Carolina, to ask, "Dee, before you had your hysterectomy were you really bloated? I can't get my pants to close."

In 1990, my gynecologist ordered a blood test and thought I had ovarian cancer. I was sent to a specialist and was soon scheduled for surgery. Instead of cancer, I had class four endometriosis which is an abnormal growth of tissue outside the uterus. I was also so sick at the time with Chronic Fatigue and Immune Dysfunction Syndrome (CFIDS), at times I wished I'd just die.

So, when Jerri called I had a strong suspicion that she was inflicted with the disease I had escaped. I felt horribly guilty that I ever thought I wanted to die. When I called Mom, while Owen and I were on a trip to Texas to find out the results after Jerri's surgery, she broke the news that Jerri had stage four ovarian cancer. My heart sank.

When I hung up the phone, I turned to my husband of fourteen years and said, "Owen, I want a drink."

Immediately, I thought what a horrible person I was to want to drink when my sister was dying. For so many years I tried to use alcohol to escape pain. My desire for a drink was just an indication of how deep that emotional pain went. At this time, I was ten years in recovery from the chronic disease of alcohol addiction.

In my recovery, there have been several times when I've craved a drink. By the grace of God and my commitment to sobriety, I have recognized those moments for what they were. I needed something to soothe me, but alcohol was not the answer. Neither was shopping or eating a dozen chocolate chip cookies. I've learned over the years that what I am really yearning for is God's strength and comfort.

2 Corinthians 10:5 tells me to, "take captive every thought to make it obedient to Christ" (NIV).

Jerri's doctor was out of town, so she was passed around to other doctors. By the time she was diagnosed with cancer and scheduled for surgery, she was so dehydrated she nearly died.

Our family decided it was best to spread out our support rather than all fly to North Carolina right away. Waiting my turn to go see Jerri was hard, but I knew it was important for Lucy, her best friend (also a nurse) to be the first one to go to be with Jerri. Weeks later, Mom and Dad went to spend several weeks with her. My turn was a long seven months later. While staying with her, I helped drive her to chemo and prepared her meals.

I considered taking Nina along with me on my visit, but I knew I would only have enough energy to help Jerri and take care of myself. Nina struggled with depression and I worried the stress of being with a dying sister might be too much for her. I wanted to focus on my time with Jerri.

A short ten months after being diagnosed, Jerri died at the age of fifty.

Jerri's Bible was sitting on the table next to the couch where Jerri spent months resting and hoping for a cure. The front was worn off, pages wrinkled from use, and miles of scripture underlined. Tucked between the pages were Billy Graham article clippings.

When I returned for her funeral, I picked up her Bible and said to my niece, "Now *this* is a Bible."

During the eleven days I stayed with Jerri before her death, we shared many memories. I reminded her of a prank I pulled during childhood that I wasn't sure she ever found funny.

The Scream

I knew when I heard Jerri's blood-curdling scream that I was in big trouble. I tried to blame Lucy who encouraged me to play the mean trick on our sister. Growing up, Lucy and I relentlessly teased Jerri for her fear of boogeymen even though I shared the same fear. Every night, she would check for the monsters underneath her bed, behind the curtains, and in the closet. I was eleven the night Lucy and I devised a plan for me to somehow sneak down the hall and past Jerri while she was checking in her closet. I quietly scooted under her bed. Just as she was going to step up into it, I quickly reached out and grabbed her by the ankle. The shriek she let out terrified me!

"What the heck is going on in there?" Dad yelled, accompanied by the heavy, foreboding clomp, clomp, clomp of his feet.

Seeing me tucked beneath Jerri's bed, Dad ordered me out of my hiding place to face his wrath.

"Lucy made me do it! It was all her idea," I cried, hoping to ease my punishment.

Speaking loudly, he said, "You're old enough to know better! Now get back to your room. I don't want to hear another word out of any of you."

Grateful to be alive, I slunk back to the bed I shared with Lucy, wondering why I had once again bought into one of her schemes.

She Had it Comin'

Jerri was the quietest of us four Weets sisters. That is, when she wasn't yelling, "You Troublemakers!" at us.

To be fair that usually happened after she had worked hard cleaning our large living room. Once she finished cleaning, she would sit in Dad's recliner to enjoy the fruits of her labor in peace. Instead, she was on the receiving end of all kinds of antics from her younger sisters including cart-wheels, handstands, and swinging from the doorway ledge and landing with a thud in the living room.

For the most part, Jerri was sweet and kind with a good sense of humor. I don't think anyone who knew her would have expected what happened one day in school when a magician was brought in to entertain us.

School was let out early that spring day in my seventh year of grade school. With high excitement, I rushed to the gymnasium with my girlfriends, Linda and Cynthia, to grab our seats on the grey metal folding chairs facing the stage. Shortly after we arrived, Mr. Magic appeared from behind the curtains and performed several acts.

When he asked for a volunteer, I was quite surprised to see Jerri raise her hand. When selected, my petite black-haired sister used her cheerleader energy to race up the portable five steps to the stage.

The magician wheeled out an ominous device.

He said, "This is called a guillotine and it has a very, very sharp blade."

He proved it by putting a head of cabbage on a curved portion on the bottom. WHAM! He let the blade loose and it swiftly shot down, cutting the cabbage in half! He certainly had my attention.

Before I could catch my breath, he said to Jerri, "I need you to kneel down and put your head on this base."

Her head was hanging over a large bucket where the split cabbage had fallen.

WHAM! I saw blood shoot out of my sister's mouth! *Oh my God, she's dead!* I thought. I was paralyzed in horror; I can still feel the rush of panic I felt.

With great drama, the curtains were pulled shut! In the silence that followed, my blood ran cold, I was frozen. I couldn't breathe, I felt like I was suffocating. I couldn't say anything. These emotions rushed through me in mere seconds.

In what seemed like an eternity, the curtains were opened to reveal my sister standing and smiling at all of us. Laughter broke out among the teachers and students, but not from me. I was so shocked she was alive, I couldn't tell anyone how I felt.

Later Jerri said, "I was chosen before the magician started his act. He gave me a capsule to bite down on and that's what made the 'blood.'"

What in the world was the superintendent or any of the teachers thinking to have an act like that!

I'd always felt badly about the time I hid under Jerri's bed. After that day with the magician—she deserved it. She had it coming!

The sight of Jerri getting decapitated wrenched at my fears and past traumas. I understood what death was and it wasn't a joking matter. I was angry at the school for hiring a magician to play such a cruel trick.

The Entertainer

Nowadays, the TV show *Dancing with The Stars* is a favorite of mine. I especially love when the dancers kick their leg in the air over their partner's head. Every time I see this, I think of my sister, Lucy. As a thirteen-year-old, she was tall, graceful, and athletic. Often, she was enraptured by the smooth dance moves she saw on our television. So, late one afternoon she decided she wanted to try to kick not one, but both of her legs up over my head. That is the type of person Lucy was; she was always ready and willing to try an athletic endeavor. At ten years old, I would have done anything for her and she knew it.

In our living room, we positioned ourselves away from the furniture for the stunt. Being the adoring and compliant younger sister, I stood as still as I could while she stood back and leapt purposefully into the air. My eyes were closed with nerves bracing in case of a failed attempt when I heard a large *KABOOM!*

Lucy fell flat on her back on the floor with a huge thud. Immediately, I panicked and thought for sure she was dead! Terrified, I ran to get Mom and Dad and found them in our laundry room. I was sure they had heard the loud thump, but to my surprise had not.

As I came back into the room with my parents in tow, Lucy was standing, bent over a bit with a sheepish smile on her face. Thankfully, not dead. The fall had only knocked the wind out of her!

Each time I watch the dancers on *Dancing with the Stars* gracefully kick a leg up and over their partner who is artfully ducking, I want to call Lucy and say, "You should have tried just one leg."

Since we are no longer energetic youngsters, she is usually in bed by then, so I don't call and risk waking her. Not always silently, I chuckle about our stunt and I think of how easily she could talk me into joining her. We have laughed about that botched dance move many times over the years.

When Lucy was a freshman in high school and I was only in sixth grade, I looked up to her as my mature and knowledgeable older sister. We would often lie in bed talking, swapping gossip and neat facts we had learned that day at school. One day, she was telling me about a film she saw in health class concerning sexually transmitted diseases. She drew me in with her excitement and detail, as she often did when telling a story.

The "sexual" part of the tale made little sense to me. Instead, I fixated on the side effects of STDs such as going blind. The more she talked, the more I wondered if I had it! Listening to her, I broke out sweating, convinced I had a sexually transmitted disease. My mind went wild questioning if I would I wake up tomorrow unable to see. Was I going blind? It was with great relief the next morning when I awoke and discovered I still had my sight! I wonder now if Lucy even understood what she was talking about.

My reminiscences of the silly times I had with all three of my sisters (there's so many more I could tell) might seem insignificant, but they created a childhood of warm memories despite the icy intrusions of one tragedy after another. I have realized that God is the one who deserves the credit, as always. He provided us with a sense of humor to help us persevere and withstand the storms.

**When life feels as if it is too much to bear,
I try to take a step back and appreciate the little moments
with loved ones.
They are the real treasures in life.**

"No one ever told me that grief felt so like fear. I am not afraid, but the sensation is like being afraid. The same fluttering in the stomach, the same restlessness, the yawning. I keep on swallowing.

At other times it feels like being mildly drunk, or concussed. There is a sort of invisible blanket between the world and me. I find it hard to take in what anyone says. Or perhaps, hard to want to take it in. It is so uninteresting. Yet I want the others to be about me. I dread the moments when the house is empty. If only they would talk to one another and not to me."

— C.S. Lewis, A Grief Observed[6]

---

[6] https://www.goodreads.com/quotes/tag/mourning

CHAPTER 7
UNCLE TOMMY

1959-1960

When Uncle Tommy died, it felt as if Billy had died a second time. Tommy Joe, my mom's youngest sibling and only brother, was born Thomas Joseph Ellefson on March 23, 1944. He was twenty-three years younger than my mom, only two years older than my oldest sister Jerrilyn, and six years older than me.

Uncle Tommy filled a hole in my family's hearts with his love and boyish energy. My Grandpa and Grandma Joe would sometimes babysit me, which allowed me to become good friends with Tommy. I adored him and was eager to please him. I came to appreciate the special one-on-one time with Tommy. It truly was a blessing.

Two days before my sister Nina was about to be born, my parents took me to stay with Grandma and Grandpa Joe in Flandreau. I was bummed to be away from everyone at home especially from Mom, so she sweetened the deal and gave Grandma Joe money to buy me a new paper doll.

As a five-year-old girl, I could spend hours and hours playing with my paper dolls, making up personalities and storylines. So, I took my shoebox full of my current dolls, plus bobby pins to secure their clothes. My sisters taught me that trick and Mom was often asking, "Where are all my bobby pins?" I was excited to have Grandma Joe take me to the store to add to my collection, but instead she decided to have eleven-year-old Tommy ride his bike to the dime store to buy them for me.

When he returned and pulled Howdy Doody Paper Puppets out of the brown paper bag, I was unpleasantly surprised. Those definitely weren't the dolls I was hoping for. Quickly, he saw the disappointment on my face. With a little persuasion, Uncle Tommy convinced me the puppets would be much more fun. I could tell he enjoyed helping me put them together. My distress swiftly gave way to happiness. I loved spending time with him, even if I didn't get the paper dolls I had dreamed about.

While we were playing, Tommy told me that my mom better be having a baby boy. He too ached from the loss of Billy. When Dad arrived one afternoon to tell us it was a girl, I worried what Tommy would think. Thankfully, my fear was needless; he handled it well and of course, came to love his new baby niece.

The next day Grandma and Grandpa took me to the Dell Rapids Hospital. Because kids were not allowed in patient rooms, they stood with me at the bottom of the steps and Mom stood at the top holding our new baby. She asked me, "Decer, can you say Denita?" I stumbled a bit on the first tries, but then I got it. "Okay, that is her name!" Mom said. Was I ever excited!

Tommy loved playing goofy tricks on us and would often get himself into harmless trouble. He especially enjoyed having young nieces who gave him a readily gullible audience. Several times he tuned the big console radio in their family den so that loud static issued from the speakers. Then, Tommy would convince us Martians were trying to contact us through the radio static. I stood there innocently, wide-eyed, and completely buying into his story. Jerri and Lucy, who were closer in age to Tommy, knew what he was up to and readily went along with it.

When Tommy was nine, he stood next to Jerri and Lucy as Dad accidentally backed over Billy. Experiencing this tragedy together bonded him and my sisters. When we went to visit, he would often take them for rides around town.

Grandpa Joe owned a produce business; when Tommy was sixteen, he drove the business truck to farm customers outside of Flandreau. I always loved it when he'd make a surprise stop at our place.

In Trent, our pond had set swimming hours with a lifeguard. No swimming was allowed when the lifeguard was off duty. But kids being kids, Tommy and his friends went swimming off hours and somehow my mom found out. Being concerned for her little brother's safety, she tattled to Grandpa and Grandma Joe when we went to visit the next day (I'm now sure it was to report Tommy's escapade to them.)

As Mom was backing out of their driveway, Tommy ran along until Mom opened her window and Tommy said, "Blabbermouth!" He wasn't mad at her; just letting her know that he got in trouble. His theatrical reaction to her blabbering gave us all a kick. Even now I can see and hear Tommy that day and it makes me smile. Our family enjoyed bringing up fun stories like that; it was healing to laugh together.

Regardless of his boyish energy and a few inclinations to bend the rules, Grandpa and Grandma Joe were very proud of him. In church, he would often sketch ladies' hats or draw doodles, so Grandpa and Grandma Joe were concerned he wasn't listening to the sermon. However, when Tommy was questioned afterwards, Grandpa bragged to us, "He remembered more than I did!" Tommy always attended their church's youth group on weeknights and Sundays without resistance. Grandpa and Grandma Joe wondered if he would have become a pastor had he survived adolescence.

November 21, 1960, was a cold and dreary Sunday. As Dad drove us to our country church, we saw Clarence, a close friend of my parents, standing by his car and waving his arms to flag us down.

Frantically he said, "Tommy's been in a terrible car accident! He's in an ambulance headed for McKennan Hospital in Sioux Falls! Joe and Esther are following it."

Quickly, we four girls tumbled into Clarence's car as Dad and Mom swerved around on the gravel road, kicking up dust as they sped to catch up with our grandparents. I thought, "Not Tommy! No, please God not our Tommy!"

Later Dad told us girls that he drove so fast that he caught Grandma and Grandpa in Dell Rapids, about a half hour north of Sioux Falls. He took over driving their car and sped to the hospital, arriving just behind the ambulance.

Tommy had been driving home from Sunday school when his car was hit broadside by a driver who had spent the previous night drinking. Tommy had been driving his old green coupe, going the ten blocks home to pick up Grandpa and Grandma Joe for church.

Upon arriving at the hospital, he was taken into surgery right away. Following the surgery, the doctor told everyone to go get some rest. Mom and her sister Beverly decided to try to sleep on the hard couches in the waiting room, keeping vigil while Tommy was in the Intensive Care Unit. My grandparents reluctantly went to Grandma Joe's sister's house three blocks away to rest. Their daughters would let them know if Tommy's condition worsened.

The nurse tried to comfort the family by saying, "Don't worry, unless you see me coming down the hall."

Hours later, Mom and Bev jumped up as they saw that nurse walking heavily toward them. They didn't need the nurse to explain; they knew Tommy was dead. The trauma to his head made it swell beyond recognition so the doctors recommended they not see his body for one last goodbye.

During Tommy's short time in the hospital, Lucy and I stayed with our parents' friend Eileen and her husband. They tried to comfort us, but they were unable to connect at a deep emotional level and thus, offered little consolation at a time when we needed empathy the most.

Eileen was a teacher at our school. One day, as we rode in her car to town from her farm, I proclaimed from the backseat, "I want to get a gun and shoot every drunk person."

Immediately, Eileen scolded me, "Now you know you can't do that," as if I had a gun and was setting out to do it.

It was just an expression of how badly I was hurting. I had promised my parents that I would be good while staying with Eileen. Her scolding me made me feel like I had been bad and that I would be a disappointment to my parents.

My grief was unimaginable. I heard them, but it was too much to take in. My heart sank. I knew it was true, but I couldn't believe he was gone forever. I cried myself to sleep that night and for many nights after.

Dad took me to stay with his sister (I'm not sure where my three sisters stayed), so he and Mom could help Grandpa and Grandma Joe. I desperately didn't want to be away from Mom, Dad, and my sisters once again. It would have been a difficult time regardless, but being away from my immediate family made it worse. Aunt Sophie and Uncle Earl were very loving to me, but they were not my parents. I promised Mom and Dad I'd be a good girl and I was, but I felt like a part of my heart had been ripped out.

I was lying on the carpeted floor in the living room watching TV when I heard a noontime news report about Tommy's accident and death. I loathed the seemingly cold, matter-of-fact way the news reporter detailed the crash and its teenage victim, desperately wanting it *not* to be true. Though I was ten years old and too old to play with building blocks, I solemnly passed the time slowly spelling out Tommy's name on the floor with the wood shapes.

The next day, Aunt Sophie took me to buy clothes for the funeral. The material of the beautiful turquoise satin-like dress complete with a chiffon bow at the waist felt soft; it looked pretty. Trying on the dress being bought for the funeral gave me conflicting feelings of joy and sadness. Tommy was dead.

Dad said that if he had lived, Tommy would have been a vegetable and that we wouldn't want that for him. It was so hard to hear; my emotions were conflicted. I wanted Tommy with us, but I didn't want him to suffer. Mom and Dad assured us that he was with Jesus now.

At the funeral home, I remember seeing Grandpa Joe distraught, crying as he knelt at the coffin sobbing, desperately wanting to open it and see his son one last time.

The day before the funeral, friends and family gathered at Grandpa and Grandma Joe's house to pay their respects. Inside, the kids gathered in the small kitchen nibbling on trays of food brought by concerned neighbors and relatives. Loved ones came from miles around. I was awed by the steady stream of people, casseroles, and sweets in their arms. They knew that even though our hearts were heavy with grief, we still needed to eat. As much as I stuffed my mouth with sweets, they could never fill the hole left by losing Tommy.

It was no secret Dad and Tommy had bonded over their mutual love for cars. I think Dad hurried to make the trade because he could not bear to drive the car he had planned to give to Tommy. Also, he was sensitive to Grandpa and Grandma Joe's feelings. He didn't want the car sitting in front of their place as a painful reminder of a future that would never exist.

In the weeks following the funeral, Grandpa and Grandma Joe morosely watched Jingles, Tommy's dog, sit by the curb waiting for him to come home. The dog's blissful ignorance turned to sorrow, as Tommy never pulled up to the curb again. Soon it was unbearable for them to watch Jingles' mourning, so they reluctantly made the decision to put him to sleep.

Jingles' death was a huge loss for us all. I don't think they realized what a painful ordeal it would be for the grandkids who loved Jingles almost as much as Tommy did. This time there was neither a funeral nor people visiting to comfort us. Today, when my dog Sophie performs tricks, I am sometimes reminded of watching Tommy with Jingles.

Tommy's death left a terrible void in all our lives. After his death, I kept expecting him to surprise us at our house, as he would often do. One time he snuck in our front door while we were all in the living room watching TV. He quietly laid down on the floor at the entrance of the living room while Mom was resting on the sofa. When we sisters looked up and saw him, he quickly put his finger to his lips to quiet us. Silently, he laid on the floor until Mom looked up and was pleasantly surprised to see him saying, "Oh, Tommy!"

Mom certainly loved her little brother and had a strong bond with him. For a long time after his death, I longed to see Tommy silently lying on the floor, waiting to surprise his sister.

Shortly after we lost Tommy, Dad had a nervous breakdown (that's how major depression and high anxiety were referred to then) and he was admitted to the hospital in a city an hour away from our home. This put extra pressure on Mom as she was mourning Tommy. It was now not only her responsibility to care for all of us girls, but also to be strong for her parents. She had to push her grieving aside to support Dad in his fragile state. Our family had always been close to each other and Dad's illness bonded us even more, especially in our faith. I tried hard to be a good girl, helpful to Mom.

In addition, Grandma Joe started having panic attacks. I couldn't understand how she felt. It was confusing to me why she would often get up quickly from the kitchen table and run outside. Years later, when my sister Jerri was dying of ovarian cancer, I became very familiar with how Grandma felt as I made my own quick trips outside, gulping for air. Every time I became overwhelmed, I thought of Grandma Joe.

For a year, it felt as if we had also lost our grandparents, too. At that time, we did not know about grief counseling. We were expected to buck up, move on, and trust God, but that was easier said than done. I hope that today kids get help dealing with their losses.

I wish I could say that the joy of having Tommy in my life for those brief years was worth the pain of suddenly losing him, but I am not that gracious. The pain was horrible, beyond anything I could have imagined. His death ripped anew the painful wounds inflicted by Billy's death.

Even though he died nearly sixty years ago, Tommy lives on in my heart. I was deeply touched by this uncle who, at times, felt more like an older brother, the one I no longer had. It was becoming increasingly hard to laugh through the tough times. With each new tragedy, I was finding it more difficult to see the humor or joy in life.

"Let your tears touch to the ground, lay your shattered pieces down. And be amazed by how grace can take a broken girl, and put her back together again."

— Matthew West[7]

---

[7] http://www.searchquotes.com/quotes/author/Matthew_West/#ixzz58cNadmtn

CHAPTER 8
HOW TO GET HELP AND HOW TO HELP

1961

During my childhood, Dad was a volunteer firefighter in our small town of two hundred, counting cats and dogs. He took his job very seriously and found pride in offering his time to help others.

Whenever the siren would scream out, he and the other volunteers would drop everything they were doing and rush as fast as they could to the fire station to find out the location of the fire and then hurry to the blaze. Often his job entailed genuine risk and tragedy, but one night it brought us all delightful amusement instead.

My oldest sister Jerri was sitting in Dad's brown recliner as Lucy, Nina, and I were sprawled out on the green carpeted living room floor with our chins propped in our hands watching our favorite action-packed television show. Dad was in the bathroom shaving with his straight edge razor.

Suddenly, we heard Dad burst out of the bathroom pulling on a button-down shirt over his white ribbed undershirt, wiping the shaving cream from his chin as he ran out of the house.

We all jumped up and sprinted to the kitchen window, vying for the best view to see what the commotion was about. We were shocked to see Dad's car tearing around the corner of our gravel road kicking up a trail of dust as he went. After the car was out of sight, we turned to each other with puzzled looks and shrugged. Anxious about missing a plot twist, we hurried back to watching our show.

Before the next commercial break, Dad strode back into the house muttering, "There wasn't any damn fire!"

"Dad, what are you talking about?" I asked. "We didn't hear the siren go off."

"Well I sure did!" he blustered.

Then it dawned on us.

"Dad," my sisters and I said in unison. "The siren was on TV!"

Letting out a sigh, he meekly responded, "Oh."

My sisters and I tried to hold our laughter in, but this drama was even better than our TV show.

Dad was naturally a humorous guy both in his actions and attitudes. I recall fondly my father's foibles from my childhood such as the TV siren incident. He loved to help people in need. One day, it was Dad who needed help. The cruel turns of life had beaten the humor out of him until there was little left but sorrow, worry, and anxiety.

The first time I learned about mental illness, I was ten years old, though in the 1950s, it wasn't called that. My mom, sisters, and I had just come home from church. Eager to change out of our church clothes, we ran to the house. I was excited to see what Dad had cooked for lunch, but instead I saw him standing in the front doorway.

His large hands were covering his face as he sobbed, "I can't take it anymore."

I didn't know exactly what "it" was, but I knew it must not be good. I feared maybe the "it" was me. Maybe I was too naughty climbing trees and not getting home in time for supper.

It was frightening to see Dad crying. He was supposed to be the strong rock that anchored down our family. Now, it appeared he had shattered and was crumbling before my eyes. So much was happening and so fast.

While Mom focused on getting Dad help, the four of us girls were ready to do anything she needed. It was important for me to be a good girl and help Mom. We didn't realize how deep the heartache of Tommy's recent death went.

Immediately, Mom moved to action. She called a hospital in Sioux Falls and made arrangements to bring him to the psychiatric ward. Then, she telephoned Dad's brother Rhine to once more come as soon as possible. Dad's other brother Hank lived down the road from Rhine so the two of them headed to Trent immediately.

When they got to our house, Dad was sitting in his leather recliner, his cheek red from pinching it. I think that he was trying to hang on, otherwise he seemed paralyzed by his anxiety. Each brother took one of Dad's arms, helping him into the car and drove him to the hospital.

My wonderful uncles were a godsend in our family's time of need then and when Billy died. Their kindness and gentleness were always a great comfort.

Once again, I was impressed by my loving family's willingness to help, no matter what.

As I sat at my desk writing this chapter of my life, I felt the need to contact an older cousin about Dad's first breakdown. I sent her a text message. I needed to know if she remembered her dad driving my dad to the hospital. When she confirmed this, the dam broke inside of me. I shook and sobbed as Owen, my husband, held me tight. Tears that had been waiting decades to fall rushed down my face. Crying gave release to the tension and fears I have carried for over fifty years. My emotions flowed easily, knowing someone else outside our immediate family remembered.

Crying gave release to the tension and fears I had carried for over fifty years.

How to Get Help and How to Help

Dad was admitted to the hospital for psychiatric care where he stayed for weeks. I don't remember how long, but it felt like forever. Mom had never driven in Sioux Falls with a population of around 40,000 compared to Trent's 200, so family members and friends would take Mom and sometimes us kids to visit Dad. Mom wasn't only dealing with the weight of Dad's illness, but also the loss of her brother a few weeks earlier. She was still coping with Tommy's absence and caring for us girls. I am in awe of Mom's courage and bravery during this time. I believe it stemmed from her deep love for Dad and her faith. She had amazing strength and compassion. Years earlier, after the death of Billy, she had made up her mind that she would have to be the strong one, but it came at a price. She didn't seek counseling, (it wasn't as common then) having to ignore her own health problems to take care of Dad and us girls and wasn't able to properly deal with the intense pain of losing her young brother.

After Dad's hospitalization, my sisters and I walked on eggshells around him, fearful of setting him off. Dad's sister felt compelled to tell Mom that if she had just kept the kids quiet, Dad would be fine. We already felt somehow responsible and her advice was cutting and unhelpful.

Years later, Dad's sister suggested that Dad had inherited mental illness from my Mom's mom, his mother-in-law. Her accusation was so absurd, we couldn't help but laugh. To be fair, she was always willing to take care of us girls. I believe that out of love for her youngest brother she wanted to fix things. Regarding the impossible claim of Dad inheriting mental illness from his mother-in-law, I wonder if my aunt felt ashamed about having a family member with a mental illness. Back then, many people were uneducated about it. It took years for us to accept it was nobody's fault.

It was a joyful day when Mom finally got the call that Dad was ready to come home. I can still hear her saying excitedly, "Lucy, grab your coat! We're going to get Dad! I need you to read the road signs for me."

Nothing was keeping her another minute from getting Dad home. It was just before Christmas and there was no better present than knowing Dad would be with us. I still get a flutter of delight when I think back on that moment. Mom had faced this challenge with courage and I continue to be in awe of her strength.

I fondly remember Dad telling us about the other people in the hospital and how much he grew to care for them. One man was an accomplished artist and gave Dad several drawings. It was another lesson on showing kindness to others.

After Christmas, Dad had to return to the hospital for outpatient electric shock treatments to help with his depression. My younger sister Nina and I got to ride along occasionally. It was helpful that Mom had an aunt and uncle who lived only three blocks from the hospital with whom we could stay. One time, I visited Dad at the hospital right after he had received an electric shock therapy session.

Before the therapy, he had been sedated. Then, seizures were electrically induced to treat or cure his mental illness of depression and anxiety. Although the treatments themselves are not supposed to be painful, it always gave him a severe headache and put him in a stupor for about a half hour. I recall him having a hard time remembering things and keeping up with the conversation. Mom assured us that he would be okay, but it was scary seeing him like that.

The summer after Dad completed his outpatient treatment was filled with family and fun. We took a family car trip to Kansas City to visit Mom's youngest sister Jackie and her family. Dad still did not feel well enough to drive the whole way so Mom, always uncomplaining, sat behind the wheel most of the trip. It was obvious even to my young self that Mom was driving extra cautious, afraid to upset Dad.

All through the trip, when she was at a stop sign, Dad exclaimed, "It's okay to go. Give her hell!"

Away we went! Dad was nervous being the passenger, but he had little choice. I don't remember any bickering; they worked as a team, as they often did to get through tough times.

Dad had several more hospitalizations for nervous breakdowns over the years. His last collapse was in 1989 when I was thirty-nine. Mom told me that suddenly he got very quiet around the house, a red flag to her. For a while, he had not been talking a lot or expressing much interest in life. When he was feeling better, Dad would often have a ready smile for others, but he wasn't himself; he was very quiet and this made her worry.

I helped Mom find a counselor for him to talk to and she suggested a psychiatrist to treat Dad. As several weeks went by, Dad was not getting any better. After much praying, a push from my gut feelings and a recommendation from his counselor Evelyn Leite, I made an appointment to visit with his doctor. I was relieved that he would see me. Respectfully, I asked the kind physician if Dad had told him about the many tragedies he had endured in his lifetime. It turned out that Dad had told him none of it.

The doctor didn't know that at the age of seventeen, Dad found his oldest brother dead, hanging in the barn. With his mother standing by his side, Dad cut Jake down from the rafters; he always carried that heavy loss with him. Or that many years later he had discovered his brother Hank's body outside in the snow after he had suffered a heart attack. Dad also didn't share that fateful day when he accidently backed over Billy or the time when he was a volunteer fireman and came across a fiery car with four children burned to death in the back seat. The doctor didn't even know about Uncle Tommy's death and how close Dad and Tommy were.

When the doctor asserted that I was a wise woman to share with him the ailments of my Dad, the last thing I felt was wise. I just wanted to do everything I could to help Dad get better. From my own counseling experiences, dealing with alcohol addiction and past traumas, I knew it was imperative to get everything out in the open, often with a professional's help.

The physician saw Dad on an outpatient basis for a short time until one day when it wasn't enough, and his shadows overcame him. Following a counseling appointment, my parents were at the house my husband Owen and I had moved into only four days earlier. Amid unpacked boxes Dad was sitting on a step stool in our kitchen; it was there he abruptly broke down and started crying.

Feeling helpless I moved closer to him and held him in my arms with my cheek pressed to his, telling him, "Dad, it's okay to cry."

He choked out, "Your dad isn't so strong now, is he?"

I assured him, "Dad, right now you are the strongest man I've ever known; it takes real strength to ask for help."

Out of our unconditional love, my family tried our hardest to get him the help he desperately needed, which we could not provide by ourselves. Mom had showed us that years before.

Ideally, our whole family would have had counseling after Billy's death and after subsequent tragedies, but that wasn't the norm back then, as I hope it is becoming today. It is probable that all of us, at some point, suffered from post-traumatic stress disorder.

Yearning for more progress, his wise counselor Evelyn Leite encouraged us to get Dad into a hospital in Minnesota. While we waited for Dad to get accepted, his physician admitted him to the hospital in Sioux Falls, where he had been treated years earlier. Because the psychiatric ward was full, Dad was put in a regular hospital room.

Dad's anxiety was so bad that he could not bear to be alone, so my husband Owen, a good friend to Dad, slept in a chair in Dad's room for the three nights before he was transferred. Owen asked Dad if the lingering trauma of Billy's death spurred on this episode, but Dad said no; it was his brother's suicide.

Dad's brother Jake had a brain injury when he was a small child living in Germany; Dad said Jake was afraid he'd be sent to war. Grandma Weets stood by her seventeen-year-old son (my dad) as he cut the rope releasing his brother's body. Once, when I complained about my middle name Helen, Dad said, "That was my mother's name and she was the best mother in the whole world." They may have already had a tight bond because Dad was the youngest child; facing the suicide together probably made them even closer. I imagine Dad's anxiety was an accumulation of each tragedy, piling one on top of the other.

When a space opened for Dad at the hospital in Golden Valley, Minnesota, Mom, Owen, and I, along with our new little puppy, drove Dad the five hours to his temporary dwelling for the next month. His old counselor explained to us that this new hospital had a wider variety of doctors that could give him more specialized treatment. We all met with the intake counselor to get information about the facility and Dad's time there.

The counselor urged us to express our feelings towards Dad. Maybe the idea was that if we all communicated well, Dad would be able to heal faster and we could all better deal with stressful situations in the future.

I took a deep breath and said, "Dad, I've always been afraid of your anger. You get so mad."

Often his internal turmoil burst out in the form of rage attacks.

Slowly, he got out of his chair and came over to me, he took me in his arms and said, "I am sorry, honey. I don't ever want you to be afraid of me."

It was a gift to hear his words of love. It helped me realize that he often couldn't help it.

It was hard for us to leave him, knowing it would be a month before we saw him again. We had to put all our trust into the physicians and professionals and their expertise at managing mental illness. During his time there, Dad attended both group and one-on-one therapy sessions. He gave both the counselor and the doctor permission to keep me informed throughout his stay. Thankfully, the therapy and medicine seemed to help him greatly.

I could relate to Dad's senses of loss and anxiety. Growing up, I was often filled with fear and emptiness, which was heightened by my own nervous breakdown at the age of nineteen. For Dad and myself, anxiety associated with loss went beyond the common malady that could be solved with some rest and the support of loved ones. It wasn't a case of just waiting out the feelings, but professional guidance was truly needed. My younger sister struggled many years with it, too.

Not only did Dad's breakdowns and hospitalizations and Mom's reactions teach me it was okay to ask for help, they taught me that it was everyone's responsibility, when you can, to help others who are in pain. (Sister DelRey, my Spiritual Director, taught me that you must first take care of yourself.) They knew sharing their life experiences, good and bad, could help others.

In preparing for Mom and Dad's fiftieth wedding anniversary celebration, a family friend shared with me how Dad comforted them in their time of need. Florence said,

> "You know, when our son died in a motorcycle accident his dad was beside himself, rarely talking to anyone. He would often sit in our backyard just staring into space. I was getting really worried, but I had no idea what to do. Then one day, as I was doing the dishes, I looked out the front window and saw your dad drive by in his pickup. I was surprised when he stopped. I closely watched him as he slowly backed up and pulled into our driveway. I guess he'd seen my husband in the back yard because right away your dad walked out back and sat down in a lawn chair next to Norvel. I don't know what your dad said but from that day on I had my husband back. And then he was able to get back to living. I'll always be grateful to your dad for that."

Me too. It was a blessing to hear how Dad's battles in life and his faith could be used to help others. No one in our family, especially me, blames my dad for backing over Billy and for his consequent breakdowns. However, my parents' absences physically and emotionally at times during my childhood and teen years left feelings of abandonment and instability.

It was hard to see a successful way of dealing with life's curve balls especially after my sisters had graduated and moved away from home. Mom did a great job of enduring, but later in life I came to question her drinking habits as well as Dad's.

Although my parents may not have been alcoholics, I learned that a drink could help you cope or rather help you ignore the need to cope with pain. I seldom saw them drink when I was growing up and I never saw them inebriated. Some laughter and fun often accompanied my drinking until the problems were not funny. It was never a subject given too much weight until it grew to consume everything I knew and loved. I didn't realize that my concentration and obsession on not drinking weren't normal either.

When I was in grade school, Dad wasn't all that keen on going to church. Often, Mom would take us girls to Sunday school and she would teach classes. One Father's Day, my parents got in a fight because he didn't want to go. Mom had given him a black onyx ring; Dad was so upset he threw the ring across the room.

I was eleven and not sure what was going on with him, but I felt scared. When they argued, I would cry in fear that my parents would get a divorce. Now being a stepmother, I can't imagine having another woman or man involved with one of my parents. It's given me greater empathy for my step-kids who have gone through that.

Dad's heart for church attendance changed over the years. He not only longed to attend the services, he was faithful also to serve on a church board and take his turn as an usher. Dad was first diagnosed with colon cancer in 1997, three months after my sister Jerri died of ovarian cancer.

Before his surgery, Dad said, "I'm not afraid, I have an angel on my shoulder."

I believed him and it was a joy to hear his claim; I was amazed by his faith. It was a precious gift to talk and pray with Dad.

Eight years later, in 2004, when the cancer returned with a vengeance Dad again proclaimed, "I'm okay. I have an angel on my shoulder."

Although he suffered, Dad was filled with faith; he knew that he was going to heaven. One week later he died.

A few years before his death he said to me, "You're just like your Mom." He didn't mean it as a compliment.

In reply I said, "Dad, I've just realized I'm a lot like you."

I was surprised when I heard his meek reply, "Yeah, I know." It was a tender moment for me because there was a lot I admired about him.

We were both good with people and each of us were challenged with a hot temper.

"*I cannot understand my own behavior. I fail to carry out the very things I want to do, and find myself doing the very things I hate. . .for although the will to do what is good is in me, the performance is not.*"

(Romans 7:15, 18)

"*You see, Alcohol in Latin is 'spiritus' and you use the same word for the highest religious experience as well as for the most depraving poison.*"

— Carl Jung's letter to Bill Wilson in 1961[8]

---

[8] https://silkworth.net/pages/aahistory/general/carljung_billw013061.php

CHAPTER 9
I JUST WANTED TO FEEL GOOD

1964-1968

Like many people in the 1960s, my family had no education about the chronic disease of alcoholism. I would later learn that it often runs in families, whether because of genetics, a culture of drinking, or an experience.

When I was little, on the rare occasion my parents would have a beer with other relatives, I would bug Mom or Dad until I got a small swig. At family gatherings, Grandpa Weets would sometimes have a jug of Mogen David wine to share, and my sisters, my cousins, and I would get a tiny glass of it. I thought it was funny when Jerri said that it made her dizzy. Not me; I liked it. Little did I know that alcohol would later capture me, take me hostage, and it would become a destructive and heartbreaking addiction.

My introduction to alcohol as a teenager was thrilling. I didn't start drinking because I wanted to numb myself. Stealing and swigging down a gulp of it was exciting! It was something forbidden, so, of course, the draw was strong.

It was the summer before I turned sixteen that my good friend Linda and I decided we'd experiment. She worked in the restaurant of the local pool hall which had a bar in the back. The owner kept hard liquor on shelves in a small, locked room across from the far end of the bar. The problem Linda and I had to figure out was how to get into that liquor room and not get caught. We thought we had an exciting plan.

While the owner was in her upstairs apartment, we perfectly timed it so that one of us would open the dinging cash register at the same time the other opened the dinging liquor closet door. The register ding would cover up our forbidden activity. We put money in the till for our selection and decided it wasn't stealing.

When we were successful, we each chose a small jug of Mogen David wine. Linda and I drank some before playing in a softball game, one of my summer passions. After drinking the wine, I felt a bit dizzy. When I fell on the pitcher's mound, no one seemed to suspect what we'd been up to.

Later that night, I thought the little wine jug was too cute to throw away, so I hid it in the hard, white Samsonite suitcase in my room. Since I didn't have a closet, the suitcase sat in a corner. That is where Mom found it a few weeks later when she bumped into it while she was putting some clothes away. Hearing something tumble in the suitcase, she looked inside.

Immediately, she yelled, "Delaine, get upstairs right now!" Her tone didn't sound like there was going to be good news.

As I got to the top of the stairs, Mom said with puzzlement and anger, "Where did this come from? Did you drink this?"

While I can remember the fear, I can't remember what I told her, but I'm sure whatever I said wasn't the truth. Now I can only imagine that Mom's anger was out of fear.

It was the beginning of me lying and keeping secrets about my drinking.

When my high school in Trent was no longer affordable for our small town, it closed at the end of my sophomore year. I had to transfer to the neighboring school in Flandreau, which was about fifteen miles northeast of Trent.

It certainly helped to have the other Trent kids there, but still my feelings of loneliness deepened as I went from a class of eight to a class of almost eighty. You'd think I would have felt less lonely in a school with more people, but instead I felt lost in a sea of strangers. I was an outsider who yearned for the familiar faces of other students and teachers. So, I did what I knew how to do, I smiled.

March 31, 1967, several months before I was caught with the jug, was a poignant day for me. Many times, over the next forty some years I would use that date as a measuring stick for the change in my behavior.

I was sitting in a junior history class at Flandreau High School when I was notified that I had a phone call. Mom was phoning from her job at the Flandreau Indian School where she was a dorm matron. Her job gave our family a lot of financial and health insurance benefits, but there was a cost. She worked many split shifts and I wouldn't see her for several days at a time. Dad had a new job traveling as a salesman for Zip Feed Mills. My parents paid me to quit my job cleaning and ironing for several families in Trent so I could be home with Nina. At sixteen, I sometimes felt like I was on my own in keeping track of Mom and Dad's schedules, making meals, my studies and taking care of Nina.

On the phone, Mom asked, "Honey, do you know where your dad is working today?"

Immediately, I sensed something was amiss, "Why Mom? What's wrong?"

At first, she denied it, but when I wouldn't give up she said, "Uncle Nantke hurt himself today."

I froze for a moment. My mind was whirling, and I needed to know more.

Mom made sure to tell me that he had been very depressed before she shared that he used a rope. Somehow, I was able to give her an idea of where to find Dad. There weren't cell phones then, so she had to try to reach him somewhere on his route.

Mom told me, "I've let them know at school that you have to leave. Walk over to Grandma and Grandpa Joe's house and wait for me to get there."

When I got to my grandparent's home, I was crying when Grandma Joe asked me, "Do you have a headache?"

A headache! Mom had told her what had happened. When Mom got to their house, she pulled me into her loving arms. We agreed that I'd take her back to work and then I would drive to Trent to get Nina from school. The grade school in Trent had stayed open although the high school merged with Flandreau. It was hard for me that Nina and I were in separate towns for school because I was supposed to take care of her.

I wanted to be the one that told my little sister. I wanted to hold her. Then, I drove out to see Aunt Hilda, my dad's oldest sister who was married to Nantke. The two of us spent some time alone. We each sat in a green wingback chair and talked about what had happened.

"I don't think that Nantke really knew how else to deal with his painful depression," I said. "I believe that God has taken him to heaven."

Aunt Hilda replied, "How did you get so wise?"

I didn't have an answer. I just knew how rough depression could be. I'd seen it before. Later we found out that Uncle Nantke had made other suicide attempts, but Dad's siblings were afraid that if Dad knew it could send him into another depression. Dad just wished that he would have had the chance to talk with Nantke and let him know he understood. Mental illness still had a stigma. People were not supposed to talk about it.

My visit with Aunt Hilda was a turning point of sorts as I look back on it. For many years afterward, I lost touch with the gut level wisdom I seemed to have had that day. Nantke's death and my time with Aunt Hilda has always been a marker for me indicating when my drinking changed and the depression I didn't realize I had deepened. While I was able to respond during the emergency, it was afterwards that my uncle's death was one more trauma building inside of me. It wasn't long after that I could no longer control the amount I drank.

**Smiling would be my way of
covering up my fear for many years.**

The school in Flandreau had a reputation for drinking. Before transferring, I decided I would not be a part of that reputation. Besides, I wanted to be a cheerleader. My two older sisters, who had been cheerleaders in Trent, didn't drink and I wasn't going to either.

I can now see how very depressed I was when Jerri graduated in 1964 and moved away from home to go to nursing school in Mitchell, SD. The following year Lucy, the sister I idolized, went to nurse's training in Sioux Falls where she lived with Jerri who was now working as a licensed practical nurse.

Both were homesick after they left for school; I hurt badly for them and for me. I wanted them to continue guiding my way, to talk over problems, be silly and laugh together. The life we had at home changed completely after they left. We didn't have family game nights unless they were home for a weekend; Mom and Dad no longer had card parties because of Mom's work hours. We didn't have the influx of my sister's friends hanging out at our house.

On the outside, I was a normal high school girl taking part in school activities, having a boyfriend, and hanging out with my friends. On the inside, I felt like I was slowly dying. Every day at the new school, I would put on a smile for the other students and teachers. At night, I would lay in bed and cry; it felt like I cried for six months.

I sobbed more the nights that Mom was working. Our family, who had been so close, was out of balance. We were splitting up and I felt hopelessly sad. I missed our bedtimes when we could each call out good-night. Recently, a cousin reminded me of this old routine: "When I stayed at your house I felt like I was in an episode of *The Waltons* (a popular TV show 1972-1981). I loved it when your family would take turns calling to each other at night from their beds that you loved each other."

I think my oldest sister Jerri started it. I smile as I remember how she would call out, "I love you, Mom! I love you, Dad! I love you, Lu! I love you, Dee! I love you, Nina!" Then we'd all follow with our goodnight loving calls to each other, but it wasn't the same without my sisters.

After all, we not only relied on each other, we looked out for each other and we sometimes pulled tricks on one another. It took me many years to acknowledge just how crushing it was to have both of my sisters move away. There had been so much other stuff going on that I didn't have time to realize how depressed I was about it. So, it was kept inside me, churning with all the rest of my sorrows. I drank to keep them down.

During my junior year in Flandreau, I looked up to Lynelle, a friend that was a year older than I. We went to high school together and sang in the same country church choir. I was sad when she graduated. Being with her made me want to be a better person.

Although I was sad to see Lynelle go, I was excited to be a cheerleader again. The spring of my junior year, in 1967, I was selected for the cheer squad. With the good influence of Lynelle gone, my behavior began to slip, but maybe it would have anyway.

Gradually I started drinking with others, going to keg parties, and sneaking a beer in The Sugar Bowl, the local hangout in Flandreau. The evening of prom, my boyfriend was angry when I got someone to get us beer. As we were walking out of my house, he "jokingly" kicked me in the butt. Not a hard kick, but enough to know he was upset and that he wanted me to come to my senses. Although I did not like his reaction to my drinking, it did little good. After all, it was fun!

The first time I got drunk, I went home feeling horribly sick. I was ashamed that I had done something I had no intention of doing. At home, I wrote in a school notebook, "I'll never do that again." Twenty-six years later, I learned that phrase is called the "alcoholic's national anthem."

The refrain "I'll never do that again" rang through my mind many times over the years.

I Just Wanted to Feel Good

Fellow cheerleader Sharon Herrick, who became my best friend forever, didn't cross that line of stepping into alcoholism. Since we graduated in 1968, Sharon and I have stuck by each other's sides through adversities, loss of siblings, health challenges, many good times, and lots of hearty laughter! Unlike my friend, my drinking caused major problems. My drinking for fun quickly turned to drinking to numb.

My senior year I was sure I was in love. He also liked to drink. When with him, I often got in trouble with my parents for staying out too late. One night, Dad showed up at a party in the street of a nearby small town during the middle of the night. He quickly spotted me and ordered me home. I was both scared and relieved when he showed up. When my parents gave me a curfew the next day, they set a boundary for me that I desperately needed but couldn't set myself. I didn't want to be rejected by the other kids. I see now how concerned my parents were for me and that they did what they could to rein me in.

When I was cheerleading, a teacher once almost caught me drinking at a football game. It didn't matter that I was risking something I loved. Nothing about my drinking made sense. Nothing! But I thought I needed that rush of ease, comfort, and satisfaction plus it was an anesthesia that I clung onto to take away my pain and discomfort. I thought I needed it to cope and to cover the pain and fear of not being good enough.

On several occasions, I took the whiskey bottle my parents kept in the refrigerator and filled an empty aspirin bottle. Then, to hide what I'd done, I poured water into their whiskey bottle to make it look like nothing was missing. I didn't know that it wasn't the aspirin bottle I was trying to fill, but the aching hole inside of me. I felt guilty but not enough to stop. I wanted that feeling again of fun, comfort, and ease.

In recovery, I've heard the saying, "If your drinking causes problems, then it's a problem." I certainly wasn't thinking straight or clearly the years I was drinking. I strongly denied that my drinking caused problems.

During my childhood, it felt as if the nation was being plunged into turmoil. The Bay of Pigs and the deaths of President Kennedy, Lee Harvey Oswald, Martin Luther King, and Bobby Kennedy hung heavy on me. Having it all televised was frightening as it played over and over. It reinforced my fears that no adult knew what was going on or how to handle anything. I didn't know either, but it made me try all the harder to control my surroundings.

When my parents were away for work, I was the one left in charge at home. I took care of Nina; I loved her, but I was tough on her when she wouldn't do as I said. When I wanted the floor swept or the table cleared, I wanted it done immediately. If Mom and Dad were gone at night, I would take Nina along with me to home ballgames. She would sit on the bench in front of me as I cheered.

My folks did the best they could, but all the trauma began to pile up in my mind and in my body. I was so scared, but I believed that I needed to act strong. I didn't want to be a problem for my parents. No one could know how inadequate I felt as the chaos churned around inside of me. I believed in God, but I couldn't and didn't act like it. I believed that I'd be in heaven one day with Jesus, but life was so often hard; it was like a mine field that I had to maneuver through. The memory of speaking wisely with Aunt Hilda played in my mind as I wondered, "What happened to that girl?" I grabbed at any chance for laughter that I found, especially with my friend Sharon.

I used drinking as a Band-Aid for my pain.

Alcohol gave me relief, an escape, for a little while. While I drank I felt brave, confident, and free. The next morning, I felt horrible, filled with guilt and shame. I always regretted drinking but couldn't seem to stop. It even started overshadowing the parts of my life that I still enjoyed. It was taking over my identity.

Ever since I was in grade school, I loved playing softball with my sisters on a local girls' team. The three older girls played pitcher, shortstop, and second base, while Nina was the bat girl. By high school, I was the main pitcher and I loved it. The summer after my senior year, I drank beer during a game and thought no one noticed, but Dad did. Going to the bathroom every inning and missing my turn at bat was a tip off.

Softball and cheerleading no longer filled me up like it had in my earlier youth. Even being up for homecoming queen my senior year didn't matter. There was an emptiness and a loneliness inside me that I tried hard to fill. Now I know that is a space that only God can fill.

Drinking was the culmination of my childhood years marked by tragedy and death. I thought drinking helped me cope with the pain and confusion of a world that seemed destined to hurt me. I decided to take the first drink and then alcohol decided for me. I wanted to be free of all the burdens, but instead I entered a bondage with alcohol. My belief that I could control my drinking was insane—each time after drinking I'd promise myself that the next day I'd do better and not drink. But then the next day, I did it again.

Mom tried to help me understand the deaths and traumas, but they were beyond understanding. I couldn't sort out what I was feeling except fear and anxiety. Now I see how impossible it was to understand all that happened; there was too much chaos that came at me and our family over and over, with no time to recover. Fortunately, there were pauses where we laughed about mundane things like the time I tripped while carrying Dad's birthday cake and all of us watched it twirl in the air, then splat on the ground.

I believe that I became an alcoholic as soon as I started drinking. From that first sip, I was hooked even though I didn't realize it. I was unaware of the power it had over me; I had no idea what addiction was. Growing up, Trent had a town drunk who would dance in the restaurant and give kids dimes and would sometimes hurt his wife. The other example was the man who drove drunk, killing Uncle Tommy.

It took a long time before I was free from addiction and gained respect for the adverse way I react to alcohol.

Recently at a fitness club, I overheard a snippet of conversation that rang true. As a man chuckled, he said to his friend, "I've heard that it's the biggest mistakes that make the best stories." I laughed to myself and thought, "Oh boy, don't I know that!"

"You can't change what you refuse to confront."
— Unknown[9]

"I set before you life and death, blessings and curses, chose life."
(Deuteronomy 30:19)

---

[9] https://www.pinterest.com/explore/alcoholism-quotes/

CHAPTER 10
TRYING TO HANG ON

1968

Mom's efforts to get Dad help when he was struggling showed me how to get help when I needed it at the age of eighteen.

In June of 1968, three weeks out of high school, I moved to Ann Berdahl Hall next to Sioux Valley Hospital in Sioux Falls, SD, for x-ray school. I was planning to be a Radiologic Technologist.

I originally wanted to be an English teacher, but I didn't think my parents could afford for me to go to college. Also, I was busy spending time with my friends. I wanted to have fun and to not think about the tragedies in my life. I wanted to feel alive!

Mom was concerned I would party too much in college, which probably was a fair assessment. She obviously knew more about my drinking than I thought she did. Of course, I didn't see it at the time because at the wise old age of seventeen, I thought

I knew everything. I was actually very sick with the disease of addiction and very immature. There were many things in my youth that stunted my maturation process.

After talking to a woman from town whose daughter worked her way through x-ray school, Mom pushed me to apply. She even wrote my application letter, doing all she could to help me succeed. Mom also applied to registered nursing school for me. After being accepted to both, I chose x-ray school because it was a year less than nursing school. However, I didn't realize it was twenty-four months straight, with no summers off. Eager to move on with my life, I chose what I thought was the quicker path. It was a decision I would soon come to regret.

Nine months into x-ray school, I was overwhelmed by constant anxiety and dread that grew every day. School exposed me to more traumas I was ill prepared for and dug up past sufferings. Inspired by my parents, I sought the help of a psychiatrist. Although I talked with him for several weeks hoping to get a better handle on my life, it didn't help.

To suppress the crippling emotions built up from the daily stresses at the hospital, I was drinking heavily. I didn't drink every day, but when I did it was too much, and I ended up even more depressed. All the while, I was unaware of the stress I held from the traumas I went through growing up. Maybe I did have shit for brains like my dad had asked when I was living at home.

The cocktail of liquor and helplessness was making me crumble from the inside out.

Trying to Hang On

My drinking escalated as life became overwhelming and I tried to swallow my fears. The horrors began my first day of school. My instructor took me to the morgue to x-ray an elderly dead woman to see if she had been strangled. I jumped when I thought I heard a guttural groan from the dead body. As my heart pounded, he laughed.

Later, he joyfully told everyone in the department. He seemed to take great pleasure in my discomfort. While they laughed, I tried to act like it didn't bother me, but it bothered me a lot. At this time in my life, I had no idea how to deal with stressful situations in a healthy way, so they compounded on top of each other until the pressure was too much for me to take.

With the morgue experience, I started school feeling insecure and unprotected. Even though I had a great roommate and had some fun with other students, school was not an easy time.

At the three-month mark, I was on weekend call with a senior student who had a bad cold. We were called to surgery to take x-rays during a hip pinning. When the senior tech said she was too sick with a cold to go to surgery, I couldn't imagine what I would do.

She gave me explicit instructions, but still I was left alone to face the surgical team with my anxiety running high. I had to correctly position the x-ray machine by crawling under the sterile sheeting that covered the patient. The orthopedic surgeon said the films I had taken were good, but when he learned I was only a first-year student, he made me retake the x-rays. It wasn't the only time someone doubted my work, regardless of the results, because I was a first-year student.

In the months that ensued, the disturbing experiences continued. I helped x-ray a body from a small plane crash. It seemed strange to me, but the procedure was required by the FFA. The body had been decapitated and had cornstalks sticking out of the neck cavity. The person's head was carried into the room in a bag. It appeared that every bone had been broken. The smell of the airplane fuel covering the corpse was beyond nauseating. I couldn't fathom how the radiologist standing in the doorway could be eating a piece of chocolate cake with that stench. Twenty years later, I woke up screaming from a nightmare in which I was transported back to that day.

Another time, I x-rayed a man's skull after part of it was ripped open when he accidently backed his tractor into a shed. I also x-rayed several people who had tried to kill themselves, one with a shotgun and the other by a pill overdose. When I decided to become an x-ray technician, I had no idea how gruesome it often was.

Every night back in my dorm, I would open my Bible to the Psalms to gain some comfort or guidance. I felt in way over my head.

One of the dorm rules was that we could go home only one weekend a month. Before I got in my sister's car for the ride back to school, I would get physically sick at the thought of returning.

Sometimes after work or class, a few students and I would go out for drinks. For me it wasn't just for fun, it was also an attempt to relieve the stress growing inside me. However, the drinking only added to my depression.

The idea to quit school was constantly on my mind as everything kept adding up. After nine months my roommate decided to quit to marry her boyfriend. I didn't know how much more I could take. I would often walk to my sister Lucy's house a few blocks away from my dorm. When I talked with Lucy and her roommate about quitting, they tried to dissuade me by listing all the expenses I would face. I know they were trying to be helpful, but I hated everything about school. Even the smell in the hospital cafeteria repulsed me. With stern practicality, my dad told me that if I decided to quit school, I'd better have a job first.

In March of 1969, I was beyond overwhelmed, seeing a counselor weekly. One day, I felt like I couldn't breathe so I went to Lucy's apartment. She made us lunch, but I was paralyzed with anxiety. I stared at the salt and pepper shakers on her table, not even capable of deciding if I wanted to season my food.

It seemed like I had hit bottom as I laid on her bed, crying uncontrollably. Lucy phoned Dad (Mom was working) who came straight to Sioux Falls to help. That day I was admitted to the psychiatric ward of McKennan Hospital where Dad had previously been a patient.

That moment marked the depths of my depression. My experiences at x-ray school were the straws, or rather the huge bale of hay that broke the camel's back.

**The depression that began as a child
was heightened with each trauma.**

At the hospital intake, I was asked how much alcohol I drank and how often. I doubt I was honest; the truth was too shameful to say out loud. All of us psych patients were marched into the main hospital cafeteria for our meals. Walking past the McKennan Hospital x-ray students, some of whom I knew, was torture. I felt like a colossal failure. We were also taken for walks down busy streets outside the hospital grounds. I felt exposed, lonely, and like a dog being taken on a walk. My walk of shame, as I saw it, often comes to mind today when I drive those same city blocks. I saw myself as a loser and was disgraced by how far and how fast I had fallen.

Several students I went to school with came to visit me. I felt their love and concern. I still have the slender blue glass vase they brought me. Of course, my family faithfully visited me. The most life-giving visit was from the pastor of my country home church.

I told Pastor Doug, "I worry about worrying. I have doubts, lots of doubts about my faith. Where is God in all this?"

He quietly listened and said he sometimes had doubts, too. His vulnerability in sharing that with me was powerful; I felt comforted and to this day, fifty years later, I still think of it. Now when doubts come, I pray, "Lord, I believe, help my unbelief."

The present presiding Bishop of the Evangelical Lutheran Church in America recently wrote, "There are some things we need to doubt so that we can come to greater faith. I think that doubt is just an intensifying of one's relationship with God."

Physically being in the psychiatric ward and being imprisoned internally by my emotions was a wretched experience. Two years later, my younger sister would be admitted to the same mental health floor with major depression. I would crawl into her hospital bed and wrap her in my arms as she laid her head on my shoulder just as we cuddled when we were younger. It was my job to protect her. It was hard to see her suffering and know how painful it was from firsthand experience.

During my time in x-ray school, I gained fifteen pounds. The extra weight added to my low self-esteem because my family valued being trim. I remember trying to squeeze into a pair of white jeans in the hospital bathroom. At my age, I didn't want anyone seeing my body.

At the end of my stay, a boy from my hometown was killed in a farming accident. He was in Nina's grade and a fellow softball player's brother. I was scheduled to be released from the hospital the day of his funeral, but I didn't get dismissed in time.

Dad came to check me out of the hospital. From there we went to a drug store to pick up my medication. As we sat in the store parking lot, Dad held my hand and his touch warmed my heart, giving me a sense of safety and hope for the future.

I realized that my parents were trying to protect me and save Dad the heartache of attending another little boy's funeral. Not knowing what was next in my life, Dad took me back home with him. Several days later, I went to the restaurant the boy's parents owned in Trent to express my sympathy. It was very important to me to let them know I cared.

I stayed with my parents for a month as I decided what to do. Ultimately, I made the decision that I would not return to Sioux Valley Hospital's x-ray program. I knew I couldn't handle it.

With my resignation came a mandatory meeting with the head of the school. As I told him I couldn't finish, I had one of my survival smiles pasted on my face. In what felt like an attempt to make me feel guilty, he told me that by quitting, I kept another person from getting an education. I felt like a loser, but I knew that it may very well kill me to return to class, so I was able to stand my ground with him.

One day at lunch, Dad and I were joking around. As he was leaving for work, he walked out the front door and in response to something silly I'd said Dad said, "You're crazy!"

Then he quickly hurried back in and added, "No, you're not! You're not crazy. I was joking."

We both laughed. Having the same experiences with mental illness gave my dad great empathy. It was helpful to have someone close to me who knew what I was going through.

I wish I could say that after I left the hospital my struggles with depression ended, but that would be a lie. It is never that simple. I have endured four episodes of major depression since that time. I learned later in life that it's okay to get mental health care; it is in the surrender that God picks me up. Back then I insisted on acting like I was okay. It was important for me to be strong and soldier through the difficulties, though I imagine more people than I knew saw through my guise.

As I tried to rebuild my life, Dad got me a temporary job in the office at the grain elevator where he worked. I considered moving to Minneapolis to be with my best friend Sharon, but I couldn't be that far from my family. A short time later, I moved back to Sioux Falls and worked as a receptionist at the clinic where Jerri and Lucy were nurses.

After several months, the x-ray technician at the clinic asked if I could work in her department. I proved myself to be a good tech and the clinic doctors urged me to go back to school. They vouched for me and assured me that I could work part time at the clinic.

I prayed long and hard over the matter. Would I be able to handle it this time? It became clear to me that if the director of the program at McKennan Hospital said I could do it, I could.

My parents worried about me returning to school. They had seen me break down during my first attempt to get an education and they were concerned how I would weather future traumas.

I faced many difficult situations when I returned to school, but instead of breaking down again, I had new coping techniques and a better support system. Margaret, a close friend and fellow x-ray tech shared an apartment with me several blocks from the hospital. I didn't feel trapped like I had in the dorm at Sioux Valley Hospital. It didn't take much for Margaret and me to laugh. Rooming with her made my life easier even though I continued unhealthy behavior.

At this time, drinking reaffirmed its importance in my life. When Nina was fifteen years old she came to stay overnight; I decided it wasn't fun unless she got to drink, too. I even tried to sneak her into a nightclub with a fake ID, but a policeman at the front door stopped us. I treasured my sister and wanted to protect her but alcohol had to be part of her night with me. It is clear to me now how inappropriate and careless my actions were, but at the time it seemed reasonable. Even though today we laugh about how the policeman chased her, I cringe recalling the bad influence I was.

Eventually I finished school, passed the required state and national boards, and became employed. However, my time on the psychiatric ward was not my rock bottom. In the long run, it did not keep me sober or heal my depression. Unfortunately, it was only the first of many temporary fixes, Band-Aids for my wounds. For years, I continued unhealthy behavior that hurt myself and those around me.

Later in life, Mom would say, "Of all our girls, Delaine gave us the most trouble."

It was embarrassing when she'd say that in front of friends and family, but I had to silently agree with her because I knew what she said was true.

"The Surgeon General's report affirms what the scientific establishment has been saying for years. Addiction is a disease, not a moral failing. It is characterized not necessarily by physical dependence or withdrawal but by compulsive repetition of an activity despite life-damaging consequences. This view has led many scientists to accept the once heretical idea that addiction is possible without drugs."

— "The Addicted Brain" by Fran Smith for National Geographic September 2017

CHAPTER 11
THE FALL

1970

One moment I was holding onto the black wrought iron railing, putting my foot forward to step down the steep flight of cement stairs, and the next thing I knew, I was lying on the ground at the bottom of the steps bleeding and confused. Around me lights were flashing. I don't recall the ambulance ride. All I remember is screaming. My screams filled the night air.

In the Emergency Room a nurse admonished me, "Delaine, if you aren't quiet, we are going to have to ask your friends to leave."

Lying on the hospital cart, I had no idea what had happened or how I got there. Panic set in and my reaction was to scream. I don't recall if my fiancé or girlfriend were allowed to stay. I only recall the pain. It is surprising I felt anything after all the drinks I had at the hotel where the x-ray convention was held. I was twenty-years-old, too young to be consuming the complimentary mixed drinks, but that didn't seem to matter to anyone, especially me. Sadly, drinking was one of my favorite past times. And what a treat! The free drinks in the convention courtesy room were provided by a company that sold x-ray films to clinics and hospitals.

The convention party was held in a large suite at the hotel in Yankton, South Dakota. Its bathroom was semi-open, with the doorway being just a curved wall to walk around. In my inebriated state, the bathroom seemed too public. I decided that I was not going to go to the bathroom out in the open! What a time I picked to be modest.

Regardless of the irrationality of it all, I asked my roommate Margaret to go with me downstairs to use her hotel bathroom. Drunk off the free booze, it made sense to us. Earlier that week my fiancé decided I should not spend money to rent my own hotel room for the night. I still wonder if that would have made a difference. Probably not.

Why did I let him decide how I spent my money? I was used to thinking others knew better than I, but rebelling at the same time. I strongly wanted to think my fall was his fault because then I could blame him for what happened. The ironic thing is that while I was in the hospital overnight, he stayed in my friend's hotel room with her and her boyfriend. They thought it was funny when they told me the next day. I didn't find any humor in it.

The following morning, I awoke in a large hospital room with several other beds separated by curtains that could be pulled shut. My face was aching and my head was pounding. When a nurse's aide walked by, I asked her for a mirror. Reluctantly, she brought me one and I couldn't believe what I was seeing. It had to be a nightmare! My two top front teeth were broken off, the jagged edges protruding out of my gums. My mouth looked bloody and the sight of it was ugly, making me want to gag. I had a huge swollen lump on the side of my cheek that was now turning black and blue.

When my boyfriend and girlfriend came in the room, I covered my mouth self-consciously. With a new lisp, I whispered to them what I had seen. Well, of course, they had witnessed it all the night before as I laid on the cold asphalt at the bottom of the steps. The nurses had cleaned me up as best as they could, but I didn't know any of that at the moment. Combining alcohol with a concussion, the whole evening was a blur. That morning, I might have still been inebriated, hungover for sure or at least in a state of confused shock.

A physician came in and told me, "You need to get back to Sioux Falls this morning; I've contacted the oral surgeon who will meet you at his office to remove those injured teeth."

As my fiancé's car passed each mile marker of our ninety-mile trip, the pain was compounded by my newfound nerves. Having anesthesia was not a possibility during the surgery because of my concussion. Since it was a Saturday morning, there was no assistant to help with the grueling procedure of cutting my teeth out.

The oral surgeon asked my boyfriend if he would be able to hold the suction tube. Trying to be helpful, he agreed to do it, but it proved too much even for the hulky wrestling coach. From my reclined chair, I saw him slowly sink to the ground. Soon he was lying on the floor and I was left alone against the pain.

After my two front teeth were removed, the doctor explained that some time was needed for the swelling to subside and my gums to heal before I could have a permanent bridge installed. I also had to wait to be fitted for a device called a "flipper" which would temporarily serve as my two front teeth.

I took the matter seriously, but I also chose to have some fun with it. The flipper wasn't comfortable to wear, so while at home I would take it out as much as possible. The gap in the front of my mouth provided my roommate and me with a few laughs. Once I got half way to work before my tongue found an empty space! I laughed and headed back to my apartment to get the flipper. Another time, I answered the door forgetting I didn't have it in; luckily, I kept my mouth shut! I laughed on the outside about my missing two front teeth, but on the inside, I was heartbroken by what I had done to myself.

One tooth that had broken in half wasn't removed. Instead, half of a false tooth was added to it. For seventeen years, I had a front tooth with a crack across the middle eliciting much curiosity and questions years later from my small grandchildren's quizzical stares as the tooth revived the decades old shame from my drunken fall.

As they stared at the crack across my front tooth, they would ask in their innocent voices, "Grandma, what's wrong with your tooth?"

The Fall

Gradually, I realized that I didn't allow myself to have that bridge replaced because I felt I did not deserve it. The physical imperfection and the public humiliation were my penance for my own stupidity. I made myself pay for seventeen years. I also hated the thought of going through the dental procedure because it required removing the whole bridge.

Some years later when I had it replaced, it proved to be very painful, stressful, and traumatizing as the dentist used a small dental hammer to tap the bridge loose. Tears ran down my face and my body clenched in fear with each tap. The kind assistant held my hand as the fall from years ago was played out in me again. She stopped the dentist to have him give me more Novocain. I was too filled with shame to ask for the extra care. I still have pain with my teeth every day, a stark reminder of the consequences of how damaging my drinking was.

A week later I was able to return to my work as a Radiologic Technologist, the humiliation really set in. The business manager told me he had photos of that night, but he refused to show them to me. He insisted the photos were too awful. Perhaps he thought they would be traumatizing. Yet, I couldn't help but wonder who all he'd shown them to.

How many people had seen me lying on the cement at the bottom of the stairs? Seeing the photos might have been a wakeup call to my self-destructive behavior. I'll never know. Unfortunately, it would take many more falls before I woke up to the truth of my life.

An insurance agent for the hotel quizzed me alone in my apartment about the details of that night.

"How many drinks did you have? What exactly do you remember? Wasn't it your fault that you fell?"

I felt extreme pressure to take responsibility for the whole situation. Ultimately, I drank the booze and I was the idiot that fell down the stairs. I was fortunate that my mother's insurance as a government employee covered my care.

In 1970, there was no accountability by either businesses or the state when it came to serving minors alcohol. No one was liable except the minor. Besides, I had no problem admitting fault. My low self-esteem is what encouraged my drinking in the first place. Everyone could see the large black and blue bump on my right cheek from hitting the wrought iron railing. This metaphorical dunce cap was a symbol to everyone who saw me that I was out of control.

When I got home from the oral surgeon's office, I called my parents to let them know what had happened.

Dad ordered, "Drive up here so we can see what you look like."

My head was throbbing, and my mouth ached as I told him, "Dad, I'm not going anywhere."

I could tell he was really disgusted with me. I can see now how worried my parents must have been. It wasn't the first time I made a fool of myself while drinking.

Once, when my parents had a family gathering, Dad placed a beer cooler in the front porch and served everyone a beer.

The Fall

I remember the hot shame as I went to help myself to another beer and Dad said in front of everyone, "Put that back! You don't need anymore!"

I felt I did need another one. It would be many, many years before I realized that alcoholism is a brain disease and drinking the first drink caused a craving to kick in. I had no clue that I had a problem with drinking, even though over the years it certainly caused me problems. It still amazes me that no one suggested I needed help, especially as my alcohol related injuries piled up. I may not have listened if anyone had tried. That is the strong and destructive power of addiction that stays with me to this day. Every day, when I run my tongue against my top front teeth, I have a powerful and sobering reminder. I thank God for helping me face my addiction from the chronic disease of alcoholism.

After I wrote this story down, I called a friend who works at a local agency committed to helping people battle addiction. I was curious how my accident would be handled today. Specifically, I wanted to know how a situation involving an underage person being given free alcohol at a professional event would be handled.

At first, I did not tell him that it was me who had the accident. My hesitancy to share revealed to me that I was still ashamed of my actions. That's a big part of why I am now sharing this ugly and unflattering story. In telling, I am overcoming the embarrassment and bringing it out into God's light for His healing. Hopefully, it will help others acknowledge, accept, and act on their own problems. That's what sharing my whole story is about, to be of service to God and to be free of secrets.

The call to Dave was healing. When I told him about the party, he stopped me when I asserted the accident was my fault because I chose to drink.

He kindly asked, "Do you think back at the time of your fall that you met the criteria of someone suffering from the disease of addiction?"

Without hesitation I replied, "Absolutely! Yes, from what I know now."

Dave replied, "Then that means you had lost the choice to drink or not. Your disease was in charge. I wish I could have been there to catch you when you fell."

His kind words choked me up and overwhelmed me with a feeling of love and compassion for the young girl I had been. As I reflected on his statement, I realized it was God who was there the whole time wanting to catch me, as well as love me no matter how badly I messed up.

In the 1970s, alcoholism was not considered a chronic illness even though the American Medical Association declared it so in 1956. Instead, an alcoholic was blamed and judged for being irresponsible, weak-willed, and stupid when they kept drinking even though it caused problems.

People suffering from addiction experience a change in brain chemistry that prevents them from making rational choices.

They are less able to control their actions, especially when it comes to drinking. I know to some that may sound like a copout. I take full responsibility for all actions and harm I caused myself and others. The destruction that can be caused by uncontrolled drinking can be cruel and I understand why it can anger people. After all, I was one of those angry people when Uncle Tommy was killed by a drunk driver.

My fall at the hotel was not the first time my coworkers saw the effects of my unrestrained drinking. At the open house for our new orthopedic clinic, I enjoyed the champagne served throughout the day as I helped give tours. Again, I was underage. Then that evening, the physicians treated all the employees to dinner at a hotel downtown.

By that time, the champagne had turned into a depressant. After our meal, the clinic manager found me sitting outside on a fire escape off the fourth floor. I was crying. It took a while for him to calm me down and convince me to go back inside. I wasn't suicidal, but at that moment the depression hit me hard and I certainly wasn't making good choices.

The alcohol compounded the distress from earlier that day when my youngest sister Nina made a suicide attempt. I felt guilty for partying while she and my parents were suffering. Beyond the guilt, I was angry she would do that to us. At the same time, I felt sorry for her and loved her. As a little girl, she would nestle on the inside of my shoulder as we snuggled and slept together.

When I expressed my frustration to Mom about my sister's seemingly selfish actions, she scolded me, "You of all people should understand!"

I knew she was referring to my hospitalization for anxiety and major depression.

There were many parties during my employment at the clinic where it should have been obvious to others and myself that I could not control my drinking. Of course, in hindsight, it is obvious, but the attitude back then was that I was foolish, irresponsible, and immature. I called myself those names and worse.

Sometimes a traumatic incident, such as my fall and the painful injuries that resulted, are enough to make a person stop drinking. Unfortunately for me, it was not enough. I saw it as a horrible accident, not an addiction and certainly not a disease. I did not even know what addiction was back then. It would take me sixteen more years to truly understand.

On the left, Dad as a teen.

September 2, 1945 Mom & Dad's Wedding Day
in Grandpa & Grandma Joe's backyard.

Sisters-Aunt Delaine Joyce Ellefson and Mom.

Grandma (Helen) & Grandpa Weets. My middle name is Helen.

Grandpa Joe Ellefson by his business truck.

Portrait of Jerrilyn, Lucy and Billy before I was born.
I stuck a photo of me in the bottom corner and
years later Denita added her photo.

Jerri comforting me on our front porch.

Mom's spirit to survive. Flood in Trent circa 1951.
Our house in the back on the left; the elevator on the right.

Billy, me in the metal stroller and Jerri and Lucy in the back.

Billy the day after his 4th birthday riding the tricycle that Grandpa and Grandma Weets gave him. Billy was bald thanks to a pair of scissors I found in a store while Mom was distracted.

RITES CONDUCTED FOR ACCIDENT VICTIM, SUNDAY

An accident occurred in Trent, Thursday afternoon, July 2, when Billy Weets, 4, lost his life under the wheels of a truck. The small boy had gone to the elevator where his father, Gerald (Jerry) Weets, is employed, and thinking he was aiding, had gone behind the truck to help push. The father, not knowing he was there, backed up and the wheels passed over his head.

He was rushed to the Dell Rapids hospital, but was found dead upon arrival. It is believed that death was instantaneous.

Funeral services were held at the house at one o'clock on Sunday afternoon with the Rev. S. G. Cleveland of the Trent Baptist church officiating. Floyd Whipkey, Jr., sang, "Tell Me The Story of Jesus," and "Jesus Loves Me." At two o'clock, services were held in Our Savior's Lutheran church in Flandreau with the Rev. R. N. Nelson, officiating. Darrell Arms acted as soloist singing, "God Will Take Care of You," and "Children of the Heavenly Father." LeWayne Leuning, Lauren Leuning, Alvin Duffert and Roger Suhr acted as pall bearers. Burial was in the Bethania cemetery. The Hermanson funeral home of Dell Rapids, had charge of the arrangements.

William Kent Weets, son of Jerry and DeVonna Weets was born on May 12, 1949, and passed away July 2, at the age of four years, one month and 20 days, having lived all of his life in Trent.

He was baptized in Our Savior's Lutheran church in Flandreau on June 30, 1949, by the Rev. Russell Peterson. Billy was enrolled in the beginners department of the Trent Sunday school and had been faithful in attendance.

He leaves to mourn his death, his parents and three sisters, Jerrilyn, Lucy Ann and Delaine; his grandparents, Mr. and Mrs. Joe Ellefson of Flandreau, and Mr. and Mrs. Ubbo Weets of Pipestone; also a great grandmother, Mrs. Betsy Monger of Jasper and many other relatives and friends.

Dell Rapids Tribune news article on Billy's death and funeral.

Me sitting on Billy's tricycle.

Me standing on Billy's tricycle.

Lucy, Jerri and me. I probably wanted to get back on top of the tricycle. Our dresses were made by Mom's cousin Judith. I imagine the bonnet I'm wearing is to cover the chop job Billy did on my hair.

Me and Kenny Olson playing in the mud puddle in front of my house.

Uncle Tommy with Jingles.

Mom at our kitchen "sink" in the 1950's.
She hauled a lot of water for dishes, cooking and baths.

The seven of us: Jerrilyn, photo of Billy,
Mom holding Denita, Me, Dad & Lucy.

Our family vacation trip to Kansas City to see Aunt Jackie's family: Stephen, Carter, Joy, Denita, Anita, Lucy, Jerrilyn & Me

An after-school photo. I'm in a dress with yellow poppet beads that I adored. Next to me are Lucy and Jerri holding Nina. The Quaker Oats Elevator, where Dad worked, is in the background.

Lucy's Confirmation Day. When the film was developed, I was appalled that one of our dogs was looking up my dress! In the back Jerri, Lucy; front Nina & Me in matching dresses.

When Jerri and Lucy were in high school, Luther League members decorated many floats in our garage for the Trent 4th of July Parade.

Trent Girls' Softball Team 1964. Back row: my sister Jerri, Linda Johnson, Bonnie Benson, Sandy Schmidt, my sister Lucy, Joyce Carlson, Manager Gladyss Janssen Front row: Ilene Lerdahl, Evelyn Ingeman, Marlene Lerdahl, Me, Francis Voss. Francis and I were in grade school and so happy to be on the team. Denita was the bat girl kneeling in the front.

Trent Pool where we girls enjoyed almost every day in the summer. I am giving Jerri's son (my nephew) Scott a ride on an air mattress.

September 25, 1982 our wedding. Lucy & Denita were bridesmaids, Owen's sons, Kenny and Michael groomsmen. John was an usher and Sylvia the photographer.

Some of the Shay kids and grandkids in front of our home in Sioux Falls.

Mom & Dad's. (Jerry & DeVonna Weets) 50th Anniversary celebration.

Sister DelRey sitting by me. She frequently came to see me when I wasn't able to sit or drive.

Owen and I August 1, 2015 at Nathan & Michaela's Wedding.

"Lord, take my weakness and may it be the platform upon which Your power shows up best."

— Joni Eareckson Tada

CHAPTER 12
IT IS WHAT IT IS

2010

For my sixtieth birthday, my husband Owen asked our granddaughter Kelsey to get the rest of our grandkids to write a favorite memory they had about me. My sisters and brother-in-law also contributed.

All the stories were touching—some bringing tears, some bringing laughter. The memory my sister Lucy shared transported me back to one of my lowest times. She wrote about my experience being strapped on a Stryker bed frame that occurred after years of back problems originating from my injury when I was an x-ray technician.

On December 26, 1973, I was required to help lift a man who was a quadriplegic. I was already fatigued from Christmas celebrations and it was the end of the day, so it seemed like an impossible task. I asked the clinic manager to get the doctor's permission to send the patient to the hospital where they had more people and better equipment to make a safer transfer.

He replied, "Doc said no. We have to x-ray him here."

My heart sank at his response. The other two x-ray techs at the clinic were pregnant and, unable to help lift the man. It was just the clinic manager and me.

Feeling I had no choice, I complied out of fear of losing my job. I felt pressured to be a good employee. Having a clinic job with every weekend off was a coveted position. At the young age of twenty-three, I didn't realize I could have refused out of concern for the patient's safety and my own. I was too consumed by my fear that I didn't even consider the safety of the patient.

I have examined that moment many times over the years always blaming myself for that mistake. Furthermore, I carried resentment toward the doctor who refused my transfer request. I'm sure it wouldn't have mattered if I had asked him directly, but bitterness has a way of sneaking in. It can still spring up once in a while toward the physician for not seeming to care about his workers' safety and at the clinic manager for his not standing up to him. I have learned to put my focus on God and not what happened.

**When these resentments resurface,
I ask God to forgive me and redirect my thinking.**

As the clinic manager helped me lift the man's dead weight, I at once felt something give in my back and pain shot down my leg. When the pain persisted in the darkroom as I was developing the x-rays, I knew I was in serious trouble. We still had to get him off the x-ray table and back into his wheelchair, which aggravated the injury even more.

On the way home, I had difficulty using my leg or having feeling in it. Over the next few weeks, I was examined by several doctors in my clinic to see what was wrong. I continued to work as an office assistant filing and typing dictation, but I wasn't able to take x-rays.

X-rays taken of my back revealed I had ruptured a disc and my fifth vertebrae had slid forward on my sacroiliac joint area. My doctor and I decided to postpone surgery until it was absolutely necessary. He was hoping physical therapy and time would fix it. Back then, doctors relied heavily on bedrest.

Several months later, I discovered I was pregnant. I told George, my first husband, that I was worried the pain medication and muscle relaxers would harm the baby. Because of my back injury, I had undergone a fifteen-minute x-ray procedure; I knew radiation was dangerous for fetuses.

When I first told my physician about my fears, he assured me it was okay. He said the medical testing and treatment shouldn't hurt the baby. Then a phone call came from the doctor who wanted to see George and me as soon as possible. The doctor said he had talked to some of his colleagues and they agreed that the "group of cells" in my uterus would be blown apart by the radiation. After being hit with this awful news, it was hard to breathe. In his opinion, I should have an abortion. However, there was not a clinic in Sioux Falls, so we would have to travel the five hours to Rapid City, SD. The physician informed us that this was due to legalities. We would have to make the appointment ourselves immediately if that was our decision.

There we sat in the doctor's office trying to comprehend an incomprehensible decision. I was in a red and white sundress ready to attend Nina's high school graduation. After a few minutes of sitting there in silence, the doctor picked up his phone and made the appointment for us. Perhaps he took pity on us because my two older sisters had worked for him so, he freed us from making the decision ourselves. I felt added distress and guilt over terminating my pregnancy especially since my sister Lucy had been trying to get pregnant. Not long after that, I was told I would be let go from my job if I couldn't do my duties as an x-ray technician because of my back injury. My husband was furious and went in to talk to one of the physicians.

Seemingly without sympathy, the doctor explained to George, "The wheels have to keep turning."

I ended my employment with the clinic feeling incredibly sad. Because of an avoidable accident, I was losing a job that I enjoyed and gave me purpose and I enjoyed being part of the team. Beyond sad, I was sick. I was sick of the drama and the unnecessary stress. I left my job with a bitter taste in my mouth.

The whole situation was a mess. Neither my husband nor I knew what to do. An employee at the orthopedic clinic told me that the radiologist who performed my myelogram was concerned my husband and I would bring a lawsuit against him. The thought had never crossed my mind.

It was two more years until I had the first of several back surgeries. I had tried whatever I could to avoid it, but along with the injury, my self-care abilities were not very good. The drinking on pain and muscle relaxation medication certainly didn't help.

Although I thought it was the answer to my suffering, the lethal combination of pills and booze made for an even bigger mess and a greater inability to care for myself.

I knew people judged me, but my snarky reply was, "Well, just let them go through what I have and then they can talk."

My back was painful, but it paled in comparison to my emotional, mental, and spiritual pain. Not only was the idea of back surgery daunting, I also yearned to have a baby. I was obsessed. In my desperation, I would poke holes in the diaphragm my husband George insisted I use. He was concerned how I would manage carrying a baby with an unstable back. Ultimately, my scheming failed, and I never told him of my deception.

In 1976, I ended up having a spinal fusion when I was only twenty-six years old. In the hospital room before the surgery, I told my family that all I wanted was to have a baby.

Steve, my sister's husband who was a farmer said, "You need to get the equipment working first."

The surgeon wasn't exaggerating when he told me that following the surgery, I would feel like a semi-truck hit me. I was bedridden in the hospital for two weeks, suffering from horrendous pain and anemia. The prescribed morphine barely made the throbbing, burning pain tolerable. A kind nurse helped me walk, and her companionship was a source of strength.

At my first post-operative checkup, the x-rays showed the bone taken from my hip and put in my lower back didn't fuse properly; my back was unstable. A repeat surgery was performed less than a year later with the same results.

My surgeon was frustrated over what to do next, so he consulted with other physicians in Sioux Falls and Minneapolis. It was decided that he would perform an H-graft fusion. Bone from each hip would be taken and packed in the form of an H covering an area from my fourth lumbar vertebrae to the bottom of my fifth vertebrae.

To give my body a better chance to fuse the bone, I was told that I would be moved from the surgery table to a Stryker bed frame to keep me immobile in order to prevent bone movement and hopefully aid in the healing.

A Stryker frame is a contraption designed for patients with spinal column injuries. Mine had two rectangular metal pieces, one strapped on my back and one strapped on my stomach. I was trapped immobile in the frame. When describing it to family and friends I would say that it was like being strapped to an ironing board. Every two hours I was flipped over like a pancake. To say it was a horrific experience is putting it mildly. I felt extremely helpless and vulnerable. My wellbeing was in the hands of doctors and nurses and the drugs they pumped into me.

One day, I was taken out of the frame to be measured for a Boston brace, a hard body formed plastic contraption extending from my hips to just below my breasts. I begged desperately for just a few more minutes of freedom before being put back on the Stryker frame. However, my surgeon didn't want to take any chances, so I was at once placed back on the frame.

Even though I had learned about the Stryker bed frame from working at the hospital, nothing could have prepared me for that week strapped in one. It was a relief to have Lucy stop in and check on me while she worked as an LPN on the orthopedic floor. She was a constant source of comfort through all my back surgeries. Her letter to me for my sixtieth birthday brought me back to that horrible time in my life, but it also reminded me of her unconditional love. I was moved to tears by what she wrote.

> *My most memorable and concerned times for you, Dee, were your "Stryker frame bed" experiences. The many back surgeries you had and lying on the Stryker frame bed—having to be turned every two hours had to be a horrifying experience. I can't imagine the fear of that and relying on someone "to do it right." I remember the many hours—days talking, being together, and just reassuring each other that it would get better. I admire you so much for your courage during those times.*
>
> *I was a nurse and worked Ortho—I knew that when a patient was prepared to be turned another team of nurses had to recheck all the setup and give the okay, but at the same time I was relying on others "to do it right"! And I remember praying, "They are trained nurses and they*

would do it right! (I also closely inspected their work.) You had many years of struggles and weakness, and then you got better—slowly and with perseverance, found a way to strengthen yourself and know your limits. You are a remarkable woman and it is so much fun to be able to do things together! We sure do love to SHOP!*

The flood of emotions that Lucy's letter evoked was beyond words. I told her how much it meant to me that she was with me through it all. Along with many prayers and the drugs, she enabled me to endure that tough week.

I continue to thank God for giving me my guardian angel sister.

Her letter was written in 2010. Since then, my health has worsened. In 2014, I suffered a bout of viral meningitis and I was soon afterward diagnosed with Postural Orthostatic Tachycardia Syndrome (POTS), which affects my autonomic nervous system. It is as if the wiring to my heart is screwed up—often resulting in debilitating fatigue, a racing heart, and dizziness.

While writing this book, I was hospitalized for acute pancreatitis. Never in my life have I had a break from health issues. I don't know what it would be like to live healthy and worry free, but despite the decades of pain, I have been blessed with plenty of laughter and joy.

I love sitting next to my sisters in church or playing Pinochle with them and my husband Owen at our home. Any time someone makes a mistake, we sisters laugh ourselves silly like we are little girls again. It's always great fun to get together with both of my sisters when I feel up for a short shopping trip or going to the pool.

When I got off the Stryker frame and into the brace, I had to wear a men's ribbed tank top underneath, smoothed with great care to prevent any wrinkles that would cut my skin. None of my regular clothes fit over the hideous contraption. Graciously, Nina let me borrow the cute maternity tops she had sewn and worn during her pregnancies. Although they were pretty, the experience was heart wrenching. Maternity clothes were meant to be worn when pregnant, not because of a back injury. Every morning when I dressed, I was reminded of the baby I wasn't carrying.

Despite the love and support of my family through the whole ordeal, this was one more experience I drank to forget. I would drink and have fun with my family and friends all the while crying on the inside. When I was alone, I would drink and cry out loud. I still did not know how to deal with my emotions in a long-term way, instead choosing the short-term solution of alcohol.

I had no idea the medication and alcohol held me in their mighty grasp.

"Laughter lightens your load and lifts your heart into heavenly places. Your laughter rises to heaven and blends with angelic melodies of praise. Just as parents delight in the laughter of their children, so I delight in hearing My children laugh. I rejoice when you trust me enough to enjoy your life lightheartedly."

— Excerpt from Jesus Calling by Sarah Young

CHAPTER 13
HAPPY DAYS

1981

It was Christmas season 1981, and I was alone. It was a year since my roommate married and two years since my divorce. I decided that I was not going to let my loneliness get me down. The "tree" I decorated the previous Christmas with my roommate Rita was a sad rubber tree plant. I wanted a real tree, so I headed for a popular Christmas tree lot. I was determined to have a joyful holiday.

Hoping to get a good deal, I explained to the salesman that I was a nearly broke, single college student. After divorcing George, I went back to school at Augustana College in Sioux Falls. In the Christmas spirit, the salesman was extra kind to me. He helped me find a beautiful tree and put it into a tree stand for me. That wasn't all! During the sale, he convinced me to go on a blind date with his cousin.

I was surprised when he said, "He's a minister."

Right away I told him, "Well, I don't think that will work. You see, I'm divorced."

He assured me it didn't matter, so I agreed to the date. If the minister was as nice as his Christmas tree-selling cousin, what was the harm?

My blind date turned out to be a tall, handsome man with dark brown hair. He picked me up at my apartment and told me that we were going to a house party hosted by his cousin Mr. Christmas Tree and his lovely wife. We had an engaging visit on the twenty-minute drive and I was glad that I'd agreed to the date.

While at the party, I met friendly couples and played games. We had a few beers and ate chislic, a South Dakota delicacy made of deep-fried meat. At the end of the evening, back at my door, he asked if he could call me again and I readily agreed.

Later that week, when I told my girlfriends about my date, it turned out that their parents knew who he was. They told me he was the minister at a church close to their parents' farms. They seemed hesitant when they asked me what I thought of him and wanted to know if I was going out with him again.

I said, "Yeah, I like him and he's going to call."

I thought they were acting odd, so I said, "Come on, spill it. You know something you aren't telling me."

One of my friends said, "He's having an affair with a married woman from his church."

Well, that was not what I had expected.

The other one quickly added, "Well, that's what we heard. Maybe he's not seeing her anymore."

I was sad to hear that. Even though the date was fun, when he called again I said no, making up some excuse. I wondered if he dated me to throw people off the scent of his supposed affair.

Now, I would tell my younger self, "Hey, give him a chance. Ask him about the rumor. At least talk to Mr. Christmas Tree about it."

I had been hurt enough in relationships and I wasn't willing to chance it with him.

It was a fun adventure and I had a beautiful six-foot tree for the holidays at a discount. The hoopla with Mr. Christmas Tree and Mr. Minister made for a great story I enjoyed telling my friends as they came over to see my magnificent tree.

The best part of it all was when I invited a guy from my divorce support group over to check out my tree. His name was Owen and he was also a group facilitator. The next Christmas, Owen and I put up a tree together and we have continued putting up trees together for the past thirty-six years.

I first met him at a celebration hosted by Catholic Family Services for divorced or widowed men and women who had completed their program. Walking into the hotel ballroom alone, I was nervous and excited. Inside, I met up with a friendly man I had previously met at a picnic. He asked me to sit with him and some other people.

As soon as I sat down, a smiling man in a blue western suit walked over and was introduced as my table mate's best friend. Owen Shay chatted and joked with us for a few minutes and then he returned to who I thought was his date at another table.

My first impression was that he was a bit too cocky. I got to know Owen more over the next few weeks as he tagged along with his friend and me on our casual dates. It was great fun laughing with both of them. Their warm spirits came at a time when I sorely needed a reminder of the joy in life.

During this time, both guys were co-facilitators for a weekly divorce support group. When I saw Owen there, I couldn't decide if he was flirting with me or just being friendly. One night we all went to a bar for a drink and he asked me to dance. I didn't realize how nervous I was until we reached the dance floor and my body stiffened up like a board. I loved to dance; I wondered what had happened to me. Through the years as we've danced together, he reminds me with a big hearty laugh, of that graceful moment.

Well, it turned out that I very much enjoyed, and still do, his hearty laugh and heartwarming smile.

After we'd dated a few months, Owen told his friend Denny his concern over our eighteen-year age difference.

His friend had a quick comeback, "Owen, how old would you be if you didn't know how old you are?"

His friend's sage advice made him realize how insignificant a number is when your heart knows the truth. Now, thirty-five years later, our age difference is more noticeable than ever, but we both agree that we'd marry each other all over again!

I am so blessed to have met Owen. I cannot thank God enough for giving me a partner with whom I have both cried and laughed. He brings me joy and humor at times when I need them most. Better yet, he often finds my faults and foibles funny rather than annoying. We also drive each other crazy at times, but that's marriage.

My good friend, Shelia, once said it best about her husband, "Sometimes, I think he's the best thing on two legs and other times I can't stand him!"

Owen has given me a family of four kids, nineteen grandchildren, and two great-grandchildren who are a great joy and love in my life.

Below are some humorous snippets of our life together that, added to the many other moments of comedy, helped us maneuver the trials and tragedies of this world.

Going to the Chapel

A look of shock flickered on Owen's face.

I thought I had asked a simple question as we were sitting on the couch snuggling, "Do you want to get married?"

Stumbling for a response, he said, "Well, what did you have in mind?"

I hadn't thought about a date but suggested, "How about next weekend?"

Owen and I had grown to be good friends quickly and always had a lot of fun together. Soon after meeting, we realized we were in love. Yet, we both had been married before and our divorces had been painful. They left scars on both us and on our families.

Owen and I each attended a divorce support group, but at different times. Then we met when we served as facilitators for separate groups. Analyzing our past experiences, we concluded we had both been immature. Our divorces made us learn better ways of communicating and helped us to grow up. These assets that we gained after our first marriages have been invaluable in our union throughout the years.

After Owen's surprise from my question wore off, we discussed the details and decided we wanted our families and a few friends to join us. Saturday, September 25, 1982, was set as the date and the wedding was to be held at East Side Lutheran Church in Sioux Falls.

Though I was a member at Our Savior's Lutheran Church across from my college and apartment, I had not yet become familiar with any of the pastors. So, we decided to have the pastor at East Side Lutheran Church perform the ceremony. He was my grandparents' pastor and presided over my Uncle Tommy's funeral many years before. It was important for me to have that personal connection.

My best friend, Sharon, came early the day of our wedding to help me with the finishing touches and to try to keep my nerves under control. Three hours before the wedding was scheduled to start, we went to the mall to find a wedding cake topper.

While we sat in my car in the parking lot, she handed me an envelope. I opened it and promptly screamed as something rattling sprung out at me. It was a rubber band wound around a wire so when I opened the envelope, it came loose and rattled wildly.

My friend burst out laughing, but when she saw how shaken I was, she apologized. I guess the idea was to cut the tension and get me to relax on that stressful day, but instead it made me come uncomfortably close to wetting my pants.

Our wedding took place on a beautiful Saturday evening, nine months after we began dating. We rejoiced with the family and friends who were able to attend, including Owen's four children and daughter-in-law.

My college roommate, Rita was also there. When I was dating Owen, she was adamant that he was too old for me—Owen was forty-nine and I was thirty-one. However, after seeing how great we got along, she made a special point to come to see me at my work to tell me she had changed her mind—she approved.

Owen's seventy-eight-year-old mother was sporting a black and blue face from a fall she had several days earlier.

When I told her that she didn't look too bad, she responded, "Dee, I look like hell."

She was direct, just like her son! My Grandma Joe said she was jealous. Grandpa Joe had died five years earlier. They were very close and it was hard for her to be alone.

As everyone was seated in the cozy white pews of the chapel, Owen and I stood together at the back ready to walk down the aisle.

With a silly grin on his face, Owen turned to me and said, "You go ahead Dee, I have to go to the bathroom."

I usually loved his humor, but at that moment I swatted his arm and said, "Oh, Owen."

He let out a delightful laugh and away we went!

The Big Bang

In June of 2006, a spring thunderstorm rolled in and settled above our town. As I backed my car out of our driveway, I heard several booming crashes of thunder. I could not believe the loud cracks exploding around me. Never had I heard it so loud! It was if lightning had struck right next to me.

Driving away from my home, the thunder sounded like it was rumbling in my backseat; I wondered if a back door was open. I slowed the car to a crawl on our quiet suburban street to check the rear doors, but they were firmly shut. I considered calling my friend to cancel our plans because the treacherous weather seemed rather unsafe, but I wanted to see Jenny, so I decided to persevere.

As I was driving down a busy main street, the sound of the thunder appeared to die down a little bit. Nearing a major intersection, a car full of young kids signaled for me to roll down my window. My mind quickly jumped to the possibility of a flat tire. If it was, I was hoping I could catch Owen at home before he left for an appointment.

I rolled down the window and was very surprised when the young lady from the other car yelled through the rain, "You have a garbage can stuck under your car!"

I mouthed a thank-you and put my hand to my face in embarrassment. I pulled off onto a side street and sure enough, our big plastic garbage can was wedged under the back bumper! With

Happy Days

some maneuvering, I managed to wiggle the muddy receptacle out without too much trouble.

I wasn't sure if the can would fit in the trunk, but I was going to give it a try. After rearranging a few lawn chairs, I stuffed the garbage can in and slammed the trunk lid. I went on my way laughing, knowing Owen was going to enjoy this story.

Later as I was on my way home, Owen called to see where I was and asked, "How is your car running?"

Assuming he knew nothing of my garbage can debacle earlier that morning, I was surprised he asked that and I started laughing.

"You won't guess what happened!" I replied and told him about the comical episode.

Curious, I asked him if he had heard anything from inside the house. He told me he heard a loud clatter and wondered if I had run into the garage door. Concerned, he went out to check and didn't see me around, but he noticed the garbage can that had been sitting next to my parked car was gone.

As he was looking around, our neighbor Wayne walked across the street and asked, "Are you looking for something?"

Owen responded, "Yeah, I am looking for our garbage can that was sitting out here."

Wayne lit up with a jovial smile as he answered, "Well, your wife just drove down the street dragging it behind her."

Apparently, I wasn't the only one to hear the "roaring thunder!"

Act Now

Who doesn't love those late-night commercials showcasing the very latest and greatest gadgets, complete with a 1-800 number for you to order from right away? Every piece of junk you didn't realize you needed is easily available. All you had to do was pick up the phone. From knives to blenders, the list goes on and on, but the best part is that if you ACT NOW you not only get the product for the low price of $19.95, but you also get the second one free, plus shipping and handling, of course.

One night, Owen and I were watching our favorite sitcom when a commercial came on for a miracle cream that gets out any stain. The energetic spokesperson had a clear glass bowl filled with water. Then he took a crisp white hankie and scribbled all over it with an ink pen. He confidently smeared the wonder balm on the hankie and dipped it into the water. Voila! Out came the stain like magic.

Mouth gaping in awe, I turned to Owen and exclaimed, "Grab the credit card! If we ACT NOW, we will get a second tube free!"

We placed the order and waited excitedly for it to come in the mail. Luck of all luck, the day it arrived, Mom and my sister Lucy had stopped by, so I had an audience while I tried out the cream.

Eagerly, I ripped into the package and told them, "Just wait until you see what this does!"

I hurried to our bedroom and grabbed one of Owen's new white hankies. Mom and Lucy watched in disbelief as I scribbled all over the hankie, exactly as the spokesman had done.

Mom said, "I don't think Owen is going to like that."

Lucy readily agreed.

I assured them, "Don't worry, it will come out. It's like magic."

After applying the cream, I dipped the hankie in the water and pulled it out to display—what? The cream hadn't even faded the ink a shade.

Out of kindness, Mom and Lucy were trying to hold in their laughter.

I again asserted, "No, just wait. It'll come out."

Furiously, I dipped, re-dipped, and then re-re-dipped the hankie, each time pulling it out with the ink firmly intact. By now Mom and Lucy were all but rolling on the floor laughing at my gullible nature.

Rather than fret over being duped, I chose to laugh with them. I couldn't wait for Owen to get home, so I could show him our magical bargain. To this day, when we see a "wonder" commercial urging us to ACT NOW, one of us will invariably say, "Quick, grab the credit card." Then neither of us moves. The laughs have been worth the ruined handkerchief and $19.95 plus shipping and handling.

Davy Crockett

On a recent fall afternoon, I was standing in the kitchen visiting on the phone with my friend when I heard a familiar scratching on our glass patio door. It was our little dog Sophie, so as I talked I went over to open the door for her. As I glanced at her through the door, I saw what appeared to be a stuffed toy in her mouth. I recently had thrown away her only outdoor toy, a duck with its wings, legs, and bill torn off long ago.

So, what was the brown thing hanging from her mouth? Then it dawned on me.

"Oh, oh my, Owen! Oh my gosh!" I managed to stammer.

It was not a stuffed toy at all, but a dead squirrel! Let me clarify. Sophie is not a big hunting dog. She's a twenty-pound cockapoo who is better suited for sleeping on the couch than catching wild animals.

Sophie was so excited to bring it inside and show me what she had caught. Quickly, I explained to my friend what had happened and she laughed as I hastily hung up the phone. With a firm voice, I got Sophie to drop the dead animal and then I let her inside.

I sternly admonished her, "You get on your bed and stay there. I'm very mad at you."

She had an innocent and quizzical look on her little face. She thought she had done a great thing that her master should be proud of her for.

I marched back to our home office and explained to Owen what had happened. He chuckled, but I didn't find it funny one bit. I knew sometimes he would shoot squirrels with a pellet gun in our backyard.

In my same stern voice, I said, "Listen, Davy Crockett, if you shot that squirrel and didn't pick it up, then I'm mad at you, too!"

Now, when I tell this story to our friends, Owen wittingly quips, "She was mad, but she didn't tell me to get in bed and stay there."

A Smile Gives Courage

Despite the good times or perhaps because of them, I had some fears about Owen dying. I've experienced many losses in my life and the fear of those to come made me anxious. At times, I feared the loss of his love and support so much it gave me stomachaches.

I can live in gratitude for what is right now and be gentle with myself when the past traumas invade the moment.

Owen has been the person who kept me going and helped with daily tasks when I was in the throes of a health crisis. Worrying about when he dies, I question, "How will I manage?" Then I realize I must go back to what I know. I know that I am loved. I know that my sisters, step-kids, and grandkids love me. I know that God has given me this moment to live and I am not to worry about tomorrow. It's so easy to forget that, especially if I am overtired and start stirring the pot of worry and fear.

Because Owen is eighteen years older than me, I have sometimes worried at bedtime that he might die during the night. At the same time, I pray that when either of us dies it happens quickly. When I have expressed my fear to others, more than one person has suggested I might be the first one to die because of all my health issues. God only knows.

A shift in my worrying about Owen's death started twenty years ago when the TV Bible teacher Joyce Meyer said, "A smile gives another person courage."

Owen and I have traversed many rough periods, mostly due to my health. Sharing a smile with each other has been a way of lifting us up and giving us the strength to continue. One morning, after hearing that advice, I greeted Owen with a big smile.

After starting several days this way, he replied, "I can't tell you how good it feels to see you smile."

I knew how he felt! When he smiled back at me, it was great. My smiles weren't limited to the morning. The joy of the Lord has stirred this up in us and we have added a greeting every morning, to complement our smiles.

Sometimes it's simply, "It's so good to see you," or "It's so good to be with you."

Owen always replies with the same phrase.

One day he surprised me by saying, "You're just glad that I'm not dead!"

"You're right!" I quickly replied.

What a glorious shift from nauseating worry to enjoying life in every moment.

What a glorious Lord!

"It's not a laughing matter, but it is okay if you laugh."
— Liz Thieman, mother of Sister DelRey

CHAPTER 14
A SMASHING BEGINNING

1983

Since I could no longer be an x-ray technician because of my back injury, I went back to school for my Bachelor of Arts in Health and Hospital Service Administration. After a one-year internship, I was hired at a nursing home near Sioux Falls. My first day began with a smash.

An hour into the day, one of the patients called me into her room. It wasn't an invitation—it was an order. So, I walked in all set to befriend her. Because she was lying in bed, I decided I would sit down in a chair next to her and visit.

Right away she yelled, "Oh no! You sat on my glasses!"

I jumped up. Not only had I sat on her glasses, I had smashed them to pieces!

"I'll take them to Sioux Falls with me right after work and I promise you I'll get them fixed and back to you tomorrow," I vowed.

Tired from my first day on the job, I drove the forty-five minutes back home to Sioux Falls and frantically ran to three different optometry shops before I found one that could repair her spectacles. The next day, as promised, I returned them to her. She was glad to have her glasses back, but I certainly was not a smashing success to her!

When I took over at the nursing home, it was in deep financial trouble, having to borrow money for the previous three months' payrolls from the corporate office. I was sent with the mission to turn the situation around. Some of the staff and townspeople were not happy about change and were quick to let me know it, as if the situation was my fault.

One of the many changes was to make the nursing home accountable for unwarranted expenses such as the large, overflowing plate of sizzling bacon and a large bowl of boiled eggs available to staff members each morning. In providing this, the residents were ultimately the ones buying the employees' breakfast. The dietary supervisor assured me that these were merely leftovers. She was only following what the retired administrator allowed.

As I struggled to adapt to my job, I felt very alone. Along with needed changes, I recognized the staff's good deeds and how the large percentage of them went beyond their duties to show love to the residents. My supervisors at the corporate office wanted me to act in love, but to get the changes made quickly. It seemed contradictory to me.

It was during this time I received a note in the mail from my mom. With it was a beautiful bookmark with the words, "In this world you will have troubles, but take heart, I have overcome the world - John 16:33." It was always like Mom to give spiritual and emotional nourishment when I needed it most. It is still the most precious gift she ever gave me.

Those words were a balm to my soul and brought a feeling of unity...*In this world you will have troubles*...I was neither alone nor unique in my struggles...*but take heart, I have overcome the world.*

I took in the promise that it wasn't all on my shoulders; God would help me through.

Over the years, I lost the bookmark and a melancholy overcame me when I couldn't find it. I guess it was lost somewhere in the shuffle of the pages of my life. The message, however, was firmly placed on my heart. I've turned to that spot in my faith often for comfort to hear the promise, a Word of hope and peace...*take heart I have overcome the world.*

The light shines in the darkness. But the darkness has not overcome the light.

(John 1:5 NIRV)

CHAPTER 15
OUT OF DARKNESS

OCTOBER 3, 1986

On December 31, 1979, a month before my divorce from George was final, I lost my temper and screamed at Mom over the phone. She only wanted to know when I was coming home for Thanksgiving, but I was hung over from a night out drinking with friends. My head was spinning, and my stomach felt rotten. I was, once again, very disappointed in myself. I felt like a total loser for getting a divorce—for choosing the wrong person to marry in the first place. Neither of us were right for each other. Unfortunately, Mom was on the receiving end of all my misery.

At that time, I didn't consider myself an alcoholic. I did know my drinking was causing problems, so I decided to try and control it. However, the lack of "anesthesia" made me even crazier. I had a hard time handling my emotions and now I wasn't letting myself numb them.

Years went by with me in a state of survival. Even after meeting Owen, I was still a mess. The weight of the world continued to press down on me and my only weapon of defense was alcohol. Going into our fourth year of marriage, I was managing two medical clinics and we had a new house and car. To some people, it might have looked like I had my life together, but it was exhausting. I had cut back on my drinking not realizing that I was striving to have some control of it.

When I married Owen, I drank less, but alcohol still controlled me. I was so worried about getting drunk that I managed to cut back to one or two glasses of wine a week. Owen said he never saw me drunk. It wasn't the amount I drank, it was the obsession of my mind and the control it had over me.

Trying to maintain control was insane. It made me tense, narrow-minded, and focused on what I could do and not on what God could do. All this time I was a faithful member of our church. I felt compelled to be in church every Sunday, hoping someday I might *get it*. I might find out the answer to what was wrong with me, but I didn't want to get to know anyone.

After the church service was over, I wanted to get out of there as soon as possible. I was afraid if people got close to me, they would find out what a phony mess I was and that deep down I was a terrible person. I was full of shame because I expected more of myself; I felt defective.

Although my life has been filled with catastrophes, some because of my drinking, I never really hit rock bottom as some with alcohol addictions do. Hitting bottom can mean that you are so low and hurt so bad that you ask for help or accept help when it is pointed out to you that there is a problem.

No matter what I went through, I had a fierce determination to live. I survived so many rough times as a child that I was resolute to get through any catastrophe, no matter what or who I harmed. I seemed to flip-flop between not feeling I deserved to live and doing everything I could to live on. I was imprisoned by my drinking—locked in without a key. I could see and feel the consequences of my actions, but I didn't know how to be free of my drinking.

The weight of the world sat heavy on my shoulders for years, but slowly, after I got divorced, I started to glimpse a better me. Meeting Owen deepened my longing to be the person that God wanted me to be. I could sense the light of possibilities growing in me and I desperately yearned to be at peace.

It was hard, but I forced my way through the darkness and gradually approached the light. My yearning brought me to a place of surrender. On October 3, 1986, I had a moment of clarity. I finally saw how I was trapped by my addiction to alcohol. I saw a new world of possibilities and finally felt hope.

The process that led to my recovery began before Owen and I started dating. While attending my divorce support group, seeds of awareness were planted when a man in recovery showed a film about alcoholism.

I felt so sorry for "those people," the alcoholics. Several weeks later, I was inspired to write a paper for my Medical Sociology college course titled, *Alcoholism and The Family*. I received an A+ on my paper and for the presentation I made to my classmates.

While typing my paper, I didn't think there was anything unusual about me sipping a glass of Lord Calvert whiskey. Although I didn't realize it at the time, I was devoted to Lord Calvert. I worshipped the bottle, all the while hungering for Lord Jesus, my Savior.

After my marriage to Owen, we became more familiar with the disease of addiction through our loved ones. First, we were asked to loan our son-in-law money for a Drinking Under the Influence (DUI) charge. I clearly saw his problem and what the solution should be, but I couldn't see it in myself.

Second, I grew worried about Mom's periodic drinking at family gatherings while somehow managing to overlook my own behavior. So, I started attending Adult Children of Alcoholics meetings. As I listened, it began to dawn on me that what others were saying fit with how I tried to handle life.

However, I still didn't understand that a big part of my problem was my thinking. It's in my nature to want to be informed, so I took a day off work to read a book on the disease. As I recognized myself in the pages, anger boiled up in me. Out of frustration, I threw the book down the hallway of my home. Later, when I looked back, I realized how often I described life as frustrating.

Not long after that, Owen called me at work to ask if I would go to an Al-Anon meeting with him. I vividly remember turning my chair away from my desk to face the window as tears streamed down my face. I could not take care of one more person!

At the meeting that evening, since we were newcomers, we were taken into a separate room for orientation. The topic of discussion was "emotional slips." Since I didn't have a stable handle on my emotions, it was hard for me to understand what they were talking about.

After the session, Owen drove us to a nearby restaurant to meet our friend Judy for coffee. She was a recovering alcoholic and had met us at the meeting. While he drove, I cried. The whole way to the restaurant tears rushed down my face.

When Owen asked, "What is wrong?"

I choked out, "I'm having an emotional slip."

Now, I laugh at my arrogance for thinking that I had a handle on the problem. My misery was confusing and uncontrollable.

As the three of us sat around the dinner table, I had a moment of clarity, "You guys, I think I'm an alcoholic."

When I said those words, I felt like the weight of the world dropped off my shoulders. The curtains blocking my view had been thrown open and I could see light. Finally, I felt hope. Judy and Owen wore beaming smiles.

Surprised, I asked, "What? Did you know?"

Judy revealed that six months earlier, Owen had come to talk with her and her husband because he was having a hard time with my neediness.

Owen explained, "I didn't know what else to do. They told me that I had to just let you suffer, to keep my hands off so that you would have a chance to get well."

It was relieving to finally know the source of my angst. I loved Owen for giving me tough love. If the situation had been reversed, I would have tried many ways to get him well and it probably would have harmed him. Whenever I think of my stormy path, I am so grateful for Owen. Going through this tumultuous time together strengthened our bond of marriage.

I was so excited about my epiphany that I wanted to tell Judy's husband, who was at home taking care of their little girl. I was so excited I wanted to tell the whole world! We quickly paid our bill and rushed to Judy's house. There we talked, laughed, and cried until two in the morning.

It was a mystery to me how I could have an alcohol addiction when I was so very careful about drinking too much. They explained to me that my obsessive attempts to control my drinking was a sign of my addiction. I was to learn that it was an allergy of the body, obsession of the mind, and a bankruptcy of the spirit.

Since I was so eager to get better, we decided that addiction treatment was unnecessary. Instead, they suggested I go to ninety recovery meetings in ninety days. In the months ahead, Owen said I didn't go to ninety, I went to at least 120 meetings.

He has often said through the years, "When you decide to do something, you really go for it."

At 6:00 a.m. the next morning, I woke up happy and with the sensation of being a small baby held in the arms of my Heavenly Father. He was gazing down at me, basking me in His love.

My determination wasn't always a positive thing, but it aided my recovery. I still strive to find a balance. I was hungry for a peaceful life and willing to do whatever it took to get well. My efforts for a better version of myself included reading everything I could find about recovery, sharing in meetings, and praying for the rigorous honesty, openness, and willingness to know God's will and to do it. I met with groups of people who also wanted or had found a new way of life, free from the bondage of alcohol. As my recovery progressed, I started visiting more with people at church, too.

Owen would tell people, "Before, she used to rush out of church, but now she has to talk to everyone."

That was an exaggeration, of course, but it was a joyful measure of my progress. God was giving me freedom to live after I successfully moved passed the fierce power of my addiction to alcohol.

For a while after I got sober, I thought more about drinking than I did when I was drinking. If someone was having a drink, I'd get inwardly impatient and wish they would hurry up and finish it.

When Mom expressed concern about my going *forever* without a drink, I got to put into use one of the first tools I was taught, "I won't drink *today*."

The slogan *one day at a time* has helped me in many areas of my life. Even though I thought I was only drinking several glasses of wine a week, I was controlled by the obsession. Alcohol and self-centeredness had imprisoned my mind. There was no room for healthy thinking. I was earnest in not wanting alcohol to cause a problem in our marriage, but it still did. For me, just eliminating alcohol wasn't the answer. I needed more than that because it also affected me spiritually and mentally.

My addiction had morphed from the time I fell and broke my teeth sixteen years earlier. It no longer seemed to cause me physical harm or issues at work, but it was eating away at me from the inside. I learned that the emptiness inside wasn't going to be filled by a drink or anything else. In facing the future without a drink, I learned from others on the same road that all I had to be concerned about was today. I often reminded myself of the motto, "Just for today," which is a useful tool for living in the present.

I was taught how to enjoy life. I saw men and women with sparkling eyes and sometimes tears. I felt their hugs. Those steps and the awesome people I met helped me in many areas of my life, teaching me, and reminding me to continually surrender and to strive to live in the moment. The process of recovery has been made up of many failures and surrenders; all of which have provided me opportunities for growth.

I have been blessed as God has allowed me to see how He has taken the many heartaches and the messiness of my life and used them to help others.

Early on, I was surprised and delighted in how often the people I met with talked about praying. I had never heard praying talked about to such an extent. So, I incorporated it into my life as I often prayed the Serenity Prayer[10] as well as others focused on surrender. It was amazing to begin to feel God's powerful transformation taking hold of me. I have come to live a life striving for openness, honesty, and being of utmost service to God and others.

Because of my recovery, I became a more faith-filled Christian, relying on God and striving to live one moment at a time. Of course, there are many times I forget. Through the help of my spiritual directors, Sister DelRey and Sister JoAnn, and dear friends too many to name, I have been able to see how God was at work in my life all those years, even when I felt He had abandoned me.

I have been free from using alcohol for over thirty years now. I am well aware everything can change if I choose to drink. I respect its destructive power.

Throughout the years I have suffered many health challenges and the twelve steps I was taught in recovery have helped me tremendously.

One day, when I was feeling down, Mom said, "Decer, I believe God gave you this program to help you deal with all your health struggles."

---

[10] See Appendix for a copy of this prayer.

It meant a great deal to me to have her encouragement and faith.

The road to recovery for me has encompassed surrender, trust, courage, faith, action, and hard work. The choice I made to turn my life and my will over to the care of God required me to look at myself and to take responsibility for my choices. In addition to meetings, I have attended counseling and four co-dependency treatment programs. My good friend, Evelyn Leite, helped me gather the courage to attend those programs. Sometimes her challenges scared me, but I trusted her immensely and I went through what I didn't want to and I grew.

Layer after layer God has brought healing. My story is not about all I've overcome and done with my life. My story is about what God has done in and through me. He took the mess of my life and has used it as a message.

When I had been in recovery for two years, I started a training program to be a Stephen Minister. In my eagerness to increase the awareness of alcoholism recovery, I asked if a counselor and co-dependency specialist Evelyn Leite could give a presentation to the class.

As I stood in the back listening to her talk, I overheard a Stephen Minister whisper to a person seated next to her, "Those people just want an excuse for their drinking."

After hearing the judgment, I vowed I would never mention my alcoholism in church. I was overwhelmed with shame as if being an alcoholic made me defective.

One day, as I was backing out of my driveway, I prayed for God to put a Christian woman in my life as a friend. I asked that she be around my age and that she share not only my problem, but also the desire to live in the solution. Very soon afterwards, I met Sue.

Early on in our friendship she said, "I have decided that I am not going to be ashamed of this disease."

I was amazed! I believe God put this beautiful friend in my life to teach me that lesson. I, too, decided I was no longer going to live in shame. Once I accepted that, I was free from the bondage of my mind. I can still have shame attacks, but I don't live in them.

Several years later, Sue gave me the opportunity to share my story at her church's Celebrate Recovery.

After I shared my story, a woman said, "I figure that if you can make it through all you have, then so can I."

Again, it was God taking my messy life and using it as a message of hope. It is my hope that in sharing these parts of my life others may be able to find healing and someday also tell their story. It is my hope that in the sharing of my brokenness, God is glorified. There have been times, like my mother who hesitated to tell about her life, when I was afraid people would think I was asking for pity. Sister DelRey reminded me that when Jesus was resurrected, He held out His hands and showed His wounds. So, for me, embracing my brokenness, leaning into recovery, and focusing on God is about having my painful and messy wounds transformed by God into sacred scars.

"Laughter is the most beautiful and beneficial therapy God ever granted humanity."

— Chuck Swindoll

CHAPTER 16
COMIC RELIEF

1970 TO THE PRESENT

Although life did not get easier for my family as my sisters and I matured into adulthood, we never stopped laughing together. Our family was close; we were taught to stick by each other.

> **It is the small but lifting moments in life that have the power to carry us through.**

One warm July 2006 Saturday evening, Mom, Lucy, Nina, and I were enjoying a delicious meal at the new steakhouse in Lake Norden, SD, eight miles from where my sisters lived. Deciding to take advantage of the beautiful weather, we walked down the block for a post-dinner stroll. After a few minutes, Mom needed to rest so my sisters sat down beside her on the steps of a store doorway. I offered to walk back and bring Mom's car to them, so

Nina tossed me the car keys. I assumed the car was locked, so as I approached it, I hit the automatic unlock button and opened the door. I tossed my sweater and purse in the back seat where I would sit for the drive back to my sister's house. After sitting down in the driver's seat, I inserted the key into the ignition but couldn't get the key to turn. I took the key out and turned it around. Maybe I had it upside down. That didn't work either.

Following several more tries I stepped out of the car and yelled to Nina, "What's the trick to getting the car started?"

After a pause, she yelled, "Lucy is going to come help you."

Good grief, I thought, and replied, "Just tell me what the trick is!"

By now I was frustrated and irritated that they didn't think I knew how to start a car.

As I stood by the driver's side waiting, Lucy grabbed the keys from me and got behind the wheel saying, "Dee, we had the same problem a few weeks ago. It's not your fault."

Determinedly, she tried as I did but this time she turned the wheel occasionally from side to side. It didn't work but she continued trying with no luck.

I was wondering if we would have to call road-side assistance. I wasn't exactly thrilled about the inconvenience of a broken-down car putting a damper on the night, but I wasn't ready to give up just yet.

"Lucy, why don't you see if you can take the car out of park and put it in gear?" I suggested.

As she reached for the gear stick and then looked down to her side, she had an odd look on her face that made me wonder if it had been a dumb suggestion.

Then she paused slightly with her hand on the shift lever between the seats and exclaimed, "Dee, this isn't our car! Our lever is by the steering wheel!"

Quickly I ducked into the back seat and grabbed my belongings and then I bent over laughing. Hastily, we walked past a few more cars over to the *other* white car in the lot. The key fit, the car started, we picked up mom, and shot out of town before anyone ran us down for attempted grand theft auto. Pleased with our getaway, we laughed our way through the countryside.

Another moment of vehicle malfunction or rather operator malfunction, occurred one spring when my family headed to the country church near Trent for a friend's ninetieth birthday party. As Owen and I reached the outskirts of town, I got a call from Lucy. She said Nina had gotten the car stuck in the mud at the cemetery while they were trying to visit Dad and Billy's graves.

When we reached my stranded family, it was clear that there was no way we were getting the car out of the mud. Nina had driven alongside the back of the graves to get closer for Mom since she was using a wheelchair. As a result, she had quite literally buried the car in the cemetery!

Lucy was laughing so hard she almost wet her pants when she told us of the trouble she had getting Mom out of the car.

"I put my arms around her and tugged but she wouldn't budge. Mom kept trying to tell me something, but I was in a hurry to get her out and in her wheelchair."

After stopping to catch her breath from all the laughter, Lucy continued, "And then I discovered that Mom still had her seatbelt on!"

Then Owen and Lucy struggled to pull Mom in her wheelchair across 150 feet of wet, bumpy grass to our van. Wanting to help, I tried to find the phone directory I had placed in our backseat a few days earlier. I was going to call a nearby farmer for help, but Owen had removed the book saying that the one inch thick eight by eleven book took up too much room.

Each of us had an opinion on what to do, but finally we all agreed to ride with Owen and me in our van the couple of miles to the party where we could ask our cousins for help. The whole ordeal was a good distraction for Mom who was mourning the recent loss of Dad from colon cancer.

Political Payback

Growing up in my family taught me to have a great sense of humor and I have strived to keep it even when I am going through rough times.

One year as election time was nearing, all media channels were filled with political ads. On the television, candidates extolled their wonderful qualities and denigrated their opponents. The most intrusive and annoying tactic the political candidates used were home phone calls. I was constantly being bombarded with campaign volunteers calling our house with their pleas for my vote.

Caller ID was not yet available, so I was never able to selectively answer phone calls to weed out the annoying solicitations. I desperately wanted some solution to this daily disturbance. One night when I was home alone, I answered the phone.

A woman quickly started explaining, "Hi, my name is Jane. I'm calling for the Democratic Party."

Quick as a flash an idea popped into my head.

Before she could continue I inserted, "I am really sorry Jane, I just can't run for office this year. I am much too busy."

She stuttered and started her comeback with, "N-no, I'm not calling..."

"Jane, really. I'm so sorry but there's no way I can run this year," I artfully interrupted.

Not ready to give up that quick, once again she tried to tell me the real reason for her call but again I stopped her, "Thanks for calling Jane. I wish you good luck in finding a candidate. Goodbye."

As I hung up I burst out in gleeful laughter. Finally, I had pay back for the years of importunities.

This anecdote may seem silly, but it stands for something so important. The fact that today I can smile despite all I have endured is a testament to the work of God in my life. Having a good laugh can be a wonderful part of that.

Richard Rohr poignantly sums up my childhood in his book Breathing Under Water. "Spiritual desire is the drive that God put in us from the beginning, for total satisfaction, for home, for heaven, for divine union, and it just got displaced onto the wrong object. It has been a frequent experience of mine to find that many people in recovery often have a unique and very acute spiritual sense; more than most people, I would say. It just got frustrated early and aimed in a wrong direction. Wild need and desire took off before boundaries, strong identity, impulse control, and deep God experience were in place."[11]

---

[11] Published March 1, 1989 by Franciscan Media

CHAPTER 17
HEALING BY GOD, THROUGH TIME

DECEMBER 1992

"Oh, my God, what have *I* done, *what* have I done, *what have I done?*" I cried out as I sat on our bed rocking back and forth, sobbing uncontrollably.

My husband Owen stood by helpless, "Dee, what can I do?"

I begged him, "Please don't leave me, please stay by me."

I felt as if I was losing my mind. We had been at a Christmas party when it hit me. Owen and I were having a good time socializing with friends when grief overcame me, attacking from out of nowhere. We were talking to a woman whom I thought was childless like me, but suddenly she began telling us about her daughter. My mind whirled and I wanted out of there. I needed to get out.

Owen looked puzzled, wondering what was going on. The grief of eighteen years was upon me once again, this time with a stronger vengeance. It wasn't new to us, but this time it hit me with a force I felt I couldn't bear. It was like a black veil had been thrown over me and was nailed to the floor, trapping me.

Owen asked again what he could do. I'm sure he was feeling helpless standing there watching his wife have a breakdown.

Finally, I said, "Please call Evelyn."

"There's no answer, who else can I call?" he asked, wanting desperately to help me.

"Try Sally."

Again, there was no answer. I asked him to look up phone numbers for several other friends, but no one answered; I assumed they were at Christmas parties just like we had been.

The thought of going to the hospital entered my mind, but I knew they would most likely put me on the psychiatric ward and drown me in pills. Somehow, I knew that was not the answer, not for this. In another situation, seeking help at a hospital could be the right thing to do. But somehow, I had an innate sense that I had to face this; that I had to go through the pain.

I asked Owen to look up the phone number for our pastor who I had been seeing for counseling. I let the phone ring until she groggily answered the phone.

"Julie, I feel like I'm going crazy. I've never hurt this badly before," I said.

She may have been groggy, but her response was immediate and spot on, "Yes, you have."

I interrupted and cried, "When?"

She compassionately said, "When you were drinking."

In the snap of a finger, in the blink of an eye, I knew she was right! For years I had desperately tried to cover this unbearable crushing pain of aborting my baby. With alcohol, I had tried to numb myself of all the anguish and sorrow that tormented me. Her comment broke the spell of guilt and shame. It brought light to the darkness. I felt relief, as did my husband. The rocking and crying ended and we were able to sleep in each other's arms.

Twice a year my heart aches as I mourn the consequences of my pregnancy terminated. That clinical sounding word was far from the agony, sorrow, and shame that tore in my heart. Each December, the anniversary month of when my baby was due to be born, and each April, the conception month it seems that my body remembers with an ache. I worked hard with lots of counseling to not get over it, but to reconcile and be forgiven by God. When I was growing up I dreamed of having three kids and teaching Sunday school, but the death of my child brought the death of my childhood dream.

Much of my story consists of the attempts I have made to get over or cover up the pain I was feeling.

I injured my back when I was twenty-three lifting a man who was quadriplegic onto the x-ray table. Five months later following the accident, a doctor ordered a myelogram to determine the extent of my injury. Later, when it was discovered I was pregnant, my attending physician recommended ending the pregnancy, telling my husband and me that the fetus would be damaged from the radiation.

Ideally, we would have known I was pregnant and told the doctor right away before the myelogram was conducted. My periods had always been irregular, and it was my first time being pregnant. I didn't think for a second it was a possibility. I would have said no if the doctor had asked me if I was pregnant, but he didn't even ask.

Numb and scared, my first husband George and I followed the doctor's advice. Because there wasn't an abortion clinic near us, we had to travel five hours. The entire experience was horrendous. Upon registering at the clinic, I was given a medicinal drink to help me relax. I felt doped up and everything but relaxed. I felt vulnerable, afraid, and helpless. My young age and insecurity made it so I couldn't see beyond this solution. George was firm in his decision that we go through with the procedure. We lived in the era where a doctor's words were trusted above all else.

When the doctor started the procedure, I cried. He told me not to worry, that it would be over soon. Through my tears I told him I didn't want it to be over; I wanted my baby. He went ahead. I was devastated.

Following the procedure, we were instructed not to travel until the next day and to call him if there was any bleeding. After we left the clinic, we drove through the pouring rain to get to a restaurant for dinner. I still remember the red and white checkered tablecloth and a dish of spaghetti on the table as my husband told me we were heading home. On the way, our little red Mustang broke down on the interstate in the pouring rain. I was boiling with anger in the passenger seat. I was bleeding and in unimaginable pain, but it didn't matter what I wanted. I guess his way of coping was to get home and get busy, so he didn't have to think about what we had just done.

As I describe my personal pain and remorse following the abortion, I am not trying to make a political statement. I am sharing this especially vulnerable part of my life in the hope it may bring comfort to someone else.

My misery stems from more than the procedure itself. I felt little control over my body in that moment in the doctor's office when George and the doctor held their power over me. I was not certain it was the right action at the time and I have regretted my lost chance to birth a child. In the months following, I visited my primary doctor repeatedly.

I complained of severe headaches that were interfering with work and finally the physician said, "This is about your baby, isn't it?"

With his words, the floodgates opened. My emotions flowed out unhindered for the first time since the procedure. Sitting in his office, I sobbed. I told him my husband did not allow me to speak about the pregnancy.

Neither my husband nor I knew how to handle this situation in a healthy way. It was beyond us. For this reason and many others, my husband and I ended up divorcing five grueling years later. It is possible that I suffered a degree of PTSD and the fact that my husband closed any possibility of discussion made it all the worse.

Although now I am strong enough with God's strength to share my story and not let the shame and regret consume me, there are still moments where the wound is unexpectedly ripped open. Several years into my second marriage, I was watching a TV talk show where a woman was talking about a horrible accident she was in.

Her husband was killed and it was discovered she was pregnant. She had broken her pelvis and due to the need for repeated x-rays the doctors recommended that she end her pregnancy. I was glued to the set as I listened to her story, our hearts one and the same. Tears coursed down my face as her intelligent six-year-old boy came out as the final testimony revealing she had refused to have an abortion. I felt like I was going to lose my mind as everything flooded back over me.

The consequences of my decision have been many and tough to bear, especially since I have not birthed any children myself. I drank. A lot. My alcoholism escalated as I spiraled downward. Alcohol, whether beer, wine or bourbon, was my way of trying to cope with the raw feelings. Feelings that were sharpened as I watched one anti-abortion commercial after another.

I felt a tremendous amount of shame. Shame that I killed my baby. Shame that I was defective. I carried the burden that I was not healthy enough. It compounded on the shame I already carried from childhood when it felt as if my family walked around with our clothes off, exposed, and asking for one tragedy after another.

Only after I got into recovery for my alcoholism did the healing begin, albeit slow. I needed to let go of a future that was never going to happen. I needed to say goodbye. With the guidance of a female pastor, I made the decision to have a naming and memorial service for my unborn child. I asked two girlfriends to stand by me as I laid a red rose on a selected baby's gravesite. Through it all, my husband Owen was a godsend! He was the first one with whom I discussed the whole nightmare. He was not only kind and gentle, but he also walked with me through my valley of tears.

Until now, I have been very selective about who I share this sacred part of my story with. I no longer live in the horrendous shame I once felt. I feel God has taken what happened to me and uses it to help others. I've shared it with several women in recovery facing a similar decision. Even though the sorrow is still there, it's not as consuming as it once was.

Last summer Owen, our thirty-year-old granddaughter, and I were watching a TV show that triggered my pain. I slowly began telling Sarah the story of my pregnancy. She listened intently as tears rolled down my face. Owen moved closer to take my hand.

When I was done talking Sarah got out of her chair, came over, and leaned down giving me a big hug as she compassionately said, "Oh Grandma, life can be so cruel."

I stood to hug her and we both wept. It was a sacred, healing moment.

Today, I share this story with you to let you know the consequences of my decision. God has brought healing. He is greater than anything—any decision, any pain, and any consequence. God has taken my situation and used it to His glory by my witness to anyone else faced with that choice. Even though I know He has forgiven me, I wouldn't wish the pain of the experience and years of sorrow upon any other person.

There are resources for those who need healing. I took part in a healing weekend through the Catholic Church for anyone affected by an abortion. To support me, my husband Owen attended the family portion of it, holding my hand.

Of course, there is still grief, but not without hope and the assurance of God's forgiveness. I know one day my baby and I will be reunited in Heaven. A few years ago, when I heard my ex-husband was dying of cancer, my first thought was, *He'll get to see our baby.*

Not experiencing the wonderful miracle of childbirth firsthand has been one of my deepest sorrows. In my youth, I took the idea of having kids for granted. When I was in my mid-teens, I dreamed of an idyllic future filled with maternal love and domestic duty. I pictured going to church and sporting events with my children, as my parents had with me. But my vision was clouded over, muddied by traumas, deaths and illnesses. My attempts to survive them were greatly affected by my disease of alcoholism.

Unfortunately, before recovery, I often lived my life in a way that hindered rather than helped make my dream of motherhood come true. It was so difficult just to take care of myself, a task which I often failed at

After I divorced George, I would often hear women in the divorce support group say, "You're so lucky that you don't have kids."

I listened as they told how guilty they felt dragging their children through the pain of divorce. In that way, it was a blessing I didn't have children with him, but at the time it made me feel empty, like there was no reason to live. I wanted someone to take care of, a purpose to get up each day.

When I met Owen, he had four kids. When we were dating, I told Owen that I could not have kids because of my four back surgeries. The orthopedic surgeon said that if I were to get pregnant, I would have to be on bed rest for the majority of the nine months. That scared me and with the way it affected my first marriage, my lack of self-worth made me assume I would not be able to find someone who would care for me for that long. Fears of abandonment ruled my life.

After Owen and I married, I had a big change of heart. I wanted kids despite the now large obstacles in my way. I even wanted Owen to have a reverse vasectomy. Without seeming to give it a thought, he said, "No." He said he had already messed up four kids' lives and didn't want to risk messing up anymore.

Beyond his reservations, others provided hindrances to my dream, too. A male pastor at church supported Owen completely. The ache for a child didn't go away but grew deep inside me.

Since Owen didn't want the surgery, I started exploring adoption. I knew the last thing he wanted was another child, but I kept searching for a way. When I met with an adoption specialist, Owen would have none of it.

At one point, we visited with the pastor at our church who agreed with Owen that more children were not in our future since we could not agree on it. When the church got a female minister, I hauled Owen in to see her hoping she would have a different perspective.

Following a long visit, she perceptively pointed out, "If Owen won't agree to adopt a child, what will this do to your marriage? Will you stay in it or not? Delaine, you have to make a decision."

It hurt to think of not being able to convince Owen, but I knew I loved him and I couldn't imagine a life without him, so I replied, "I'll stay."

"So then, you have to agree that you won't bring this topic up again with him. Agreed?" the minister pressed.

Soon after making my decision, I became a grandma. When our daughter-in-law Jean was pregnant, she asked if I would let her children call me Grandma Dee. Not step-grandma, but simply Grandma Dee. Over the years, I have welcomed and thoroughly enjoyed being a grandma to each precious baby I have held in my arms. I even had the joy of being in the delivery room for the birth of a little ginger-haired grandson. Being a part of this wonderful family has included trials and much joy!

A moment that accurately captures the joy and humor my grandchildren have brought me is when I asked my four-year-old grandson Noah how old he thought I was. As I worked on a crossword puzzle, I heard him say something about the age of his brothers. So, I thought I'd quiz him. He got the ages of both brothers right and I moved on to his parents.

His dad, who had just arrived home from a tour in Iraq, had recently celebrated his fortieth birthday, so it was no surprise he got his age correct. When I asked about his mom, he guessed maybe forty-one. She was turning thirty-eight the next week and I could not wait to tell her Noah's guess. Amused by this game, I asked how old he thought I was.

Without much hesitation he replied, "Hmm. . .one hundred some."

I broke out laughing as he stared up at me innocently. Out of my pain and grief, God brought life. It came in a different form from what I expected. I now have four children, nineteen grandchildren, and two great-grandchildren. As our family grows, I strive to enjoy every minute of it.

We have trials as all families do, but in the end, I got a treasure beyond anything I could have imagined.

It has been a rough road with many speed bumps. They have seen me messy, broken, angry, peevish, and soaked in self-pity, but they love me anyway. It was and still is a humbling journey. They've also seen me loving, funny, faith-filled, and laughing.

In our family, there is so much laughter even over the silliest things. They tease me about my quirks and foibles and I love it. The love I have for my grandchildren overwhelms my heart.

"A smile costs nothing but gives much. It enriches those who receive without making poorer those who give. It takes but a moment, but the memory of it sometimes lasts forever. None is so rich or mighty that she cannot get along without it and none is so poor that she cannot be made rich by it. Yet a smile cannot be bought, begged, borrowed, or stolen, for it is something that is of no value to anyone until it is given away."

— Author Unknown[12]

---

[12] http://www.searchquotes.com/search/Christian_Smile/#ixzz5A8QX499z

CHAPTER 18
WHEN SHE SMILED

MAY 2007

"**S**he can light the world up with her smile," boomed the theme song from the popular 1970s sitcom *The Mary Tyler Moore Show*.

Like many other women at that time, I wanted to be just like Mary. She was beautiful and kind; she made mistakes but she was loved in spite of them. Mary could light up the world with her smile, but she had nothing on my mom's smile.

Her smile was so radiant it was like a ray of sunshine bursting through the clouds on a rainy day. It was so enchanting that I not only felt the warmth on my face, but also in my heart. The older she got, the more brilliant it shone. Mom's smile would outshine Mary's any day.

Sometimes when visiting Mom at her home, she would be napping. The smile I received when I roused her was full of love. As she became more physically vulnerable, she looked up at me with such child-like glee and sweetness, greeting me, "Hi, Decer."

Hearing that filled me with warmth. On the phone sometimes she'd say, "Hi Desaw" and I'd reply, "Hello Mudder." I still treasure the bits of love and silliness we shared.

One day, I surprised Mom during lunch at her nursing home. She gave me the tightest and longest hug as she whispered, "Oh, Decer, you're here! I have missed you." How I had missed her, too.

In 2004, when she was eighty-six years old, Dad died of colon cancer. He'd first been diagnosed eight years earlier, only three months after my oldest sister Jerri died of ovarian cancer. A few weeks after his passing, Mom still managed a warm smile when greeting other residents in the assisted living center she had moved into following his death.

Despite her pain, there was something pure and kind within her that couldn't help but shine through. I know her smile came from deep within her; it wasn't an artificially pasted on grin, but rather it came from the Creator Himself.

When Mom smiled, it was as if God was sending a message that everything would be all right.

When I was younger, I remember going through a stage where I absolutely did not want to be anything like my mom. But for many decades now, I find myself enjoying that I am becoming more and more like her. It's comical seeing some of her traits in my sisters, too. It's always fun when my sisters and I share silly stories about Mom. She truly was the mom who could light up the world with her smile.

When She Smiled

I don't mean to paint the picture that she was always smiling. That just wouldn't be healthy. Over the years, I saw Mom angry, sad, disgusted, disappointed, and horrified. When I asked her and Dad if they would go to a counseling session with me after the flashback of Billy's accident, the momentary look on Mom's face was ghastly. I told them the counselor had suggested it, but I dropped the issue as soon as I saw Mom's face.

Over the years, even though Mom dealt with one health problem after another, her spirit was often still joyful, but, of course, not always. When you have as many health problems as Mom and I have had, there is a constant cycle of grief. Sometimes she would get stuck in her sorrow, much as I have at times. While I like to recall her good humor and her smile, it's helpful for me to recall her sternness when she would lay down the law and refuse to put up with my shenanigans.

Owen and I enjoy recalling fun times with my parents. In 1991, my husband and I attended the Prairie Repertory Theater's production of *The Music Man* with them. Mom especially liked the lead actor's portrayal of Professor Hill. At the end of the show, we wanted to get in line to shake hands with the cast members. That didn't appeal to Dad or Owen, so they went outside.

After we went through the line and got on the elevator, we talked excitedly about what a great job the actors had done and how we were glad we got the opportunity to thank them.

Mom turned to me and said in a serious tone, "You know, I think Professor Hill almost kissed me."

Surprised, I asked with a chuckle, "What would you have done?"

Without hesitation she smiled and said, "I would have let him!"

That was Mom. No matter what she endured, she stayed truly young at heart!

One time, I painted a pink rose on a black background in an oil painting class.

When my sisters and Mom came to the house Mom said, "The girls told me you painted a rose. I want to see it, but let's eat first."

In the middle of the meal she brought it up again and I said, "Why don't we wait until we're finished eating."

When she was done eating, I offered her my arm to help her walk down the hallway where she could finally see my masterpiece.

As we stood looking at the painting Mom slowly said, "Oh my. . .what a *beautiful* frame."

I burst out laughing! Mom didn't even realize what she'd said. Later, she was surprised when we pointed out the comedy in her statement.

When we teased her about it she asked, "Did I really say that?"

Mother's Day, 2007

Mother's Day 2007 started off uneasily. When Owen and I walked into the nursing home in Estelline, Mom wasn't sitting out in her doorway watching for us like she usually did. So, I walked into her room and knelt in front of her wheelchair. I saw that she was slightly confused and looked terribly tired. It was disappointing and worrisome. Usually, she would great us with dancing eyes and a sparkling smile, excited to see us.

I had brought her some small things for Mother's Day. She was always delighted to receive gifts. Unfortunately, her confused state made it hard for her to enjoy the stained-glass window hanging, a box of wine for her usual evening glass, a geranium plant for outside her window, and a package of her favorite black licorice.

At her request, I also brought a small cloth doll I had previously sewn for her seventieth birthday.

As Mom held it, she said, "Oh, yes," pausing as if searching for a connection. With a look of confusion, she said, "I made this for your fortieth birthday."

My heart sank as her eyes glossed over. It seemed I was losing my mom as she sat right in front of me.

It was almost lunch time, so Owen wheeled Mom down the hall into the dining room Lucy reserved for our Mother's Day meal. Lucy worked at the nursing home as a registered nurse. Mom had terrible difficulty eating, often bringing the fork up and making several attempts to find her mouth. It took a lot to restrain myself from taking her fork to feed her myself, but when I asked if she wanted help she insisted she could do it. By the time she made it to her dessert, she had become more lucid and was able to really enjoy the lemon meringue pie, wishing for a second piece.

After lunch, Owen wheeled Mom outside to the courtyard so she could have a cigarette. As we sat facing her room, she admired the beautiful baskets of flowers and the gold finches that flocked to her window bird feeder.

It was a gorgeous day and more than once Mom mentioned how much she loved being outside. She sat munching on the licorice I brought her, making her mouth and tongue turn black. She looked comical and sweet at the same time. I asked if she wanted to go in and take a short nap before coffee time, but she said emphatically that she wanted to stay outside.

Around three o'clock, we gathered with Mom's fellow residents and their guests in the dining room. Margie, Mom's best friend since moving there, joined us at the table as she usually did when we visited. I thought it was special and hopeful that even in her eighties, Mom was open to having a new close friend.

Mom was excited the treat that day was an ice cream sundae. After eating, exhaustion quickly hit Mom. Nina and her husband Bryan brought Mom back to her room while Owen and I went over to Lucy's to drop something off.

When I returned, Nina told me, "Mom is really tired and said she just wants to sleep."

She had a hard time keeping her eyes open when I crawled onto her bed.

That's when she said, "I'm so tired. Don't think for one minute that I don't love you because I do."

I hugged her tight, "I know Mom, I love you too, very much."

Those would be the last words we exchanged.

The next day at 5 p.m., just before I was leaving for a meeting, the phone rang. It was Lucy telling me that Mom's blood pressure had hit a real low then shot way up. To include me in Mom's care, Lucy asked if I thought we should send her to the hospital so they could try to stabilize her. Lucy was concerned that Mom had suffered several small seizures because of the swings in her blood pressure. We three sisters agreed that Mom had suffered *enough* in her life, it was time to let her go. As soon as I hung up, I told Owen we needed to drive up to the nursing home right away.

When we reached her bedside, we tried to interact with her, but she was not responding.

Then Owen greeted her with a kiss on her forehead and her old high school nickname, "Hi Bonesy, it's me Owen."

We were surprised when Mom let out a laugh! After that she didn't respond again.

Mom is the person who taught me that no matter what life throws at you, you can often find a way to laugh. It may take some time, but the laughter will come. Mom endured so much during lifetime. I am still in awe of her ability to keep living despite the heavy burdens placed on her shoulders.

It was her smile and gift of laughter that gave her a reprieve from her troubles and helped our family. Sometimes humor was hard to come by, but we got through whatever tough thing hit us and found light in the dark. Life could come crashing down, but eventually we would find something to laugh about.

"If God is found in our hard times, then all of life, no matter how apparently insignificant or difficult, can open us to God's work among us. To be grateful does not mean repressing our remembered hurts. But as we come to God with our hurts—honestly, not superficially—something life changing can begin slowly to happen. We discover how God is the One who invites us to healing. We realize that any dance of celebration must weave both the sorrows and the blessings into a joyful step."

— Turn My Mourning Into Dancing
by Henri Nouwen

CHAPTER 19
FAITH

For it is by grace you have been saved, through faith—and this is not from yourselves, it is the gift of God—not by works, so that no one can boast. For we are God's handiwork, created in Christ Jesus to do good works, which God prepared in advance for us to do.

(Ephesians 2:8-10 NIV)

Ephesians 2:8-10 are what I call my life verses. They remind me of the amazing gift of faith God has given me by His grace through the death and resurrection of Jesus Christ.

When I was growing up I thought that I had to produce faith and I had to be good enough to earn God's love by behaving well. Again and again, I felt like I was failing. It was a relief to realize that the beautiful gold-paper-wrapped gift of God's love only needed to be unwrapped and accepted. He will always guide me, if I pay attention and listen and quit trying to direct my life and everyone else's.

For a long time, I couldn't stop beating myself up for my sins and my alcohol addiction. I carried shame with me wherever I went. I was so headstrong that I thought the only way through life was to steamroll my way with sheer determination, no matter what happened.

When I was young, I judged others too easily, so it was very humbling when I was the one who failed over and over. Those moments of brokenness and vulnerability brought me to my knees and I finally recognized I was not in control. Of course, my helplessness did not feel good at the time nor has it ever, but it gives me freedom. God brings light to my darkness.

Sharing my brokenness with others I trust makes my surrendering even more empowering and healing. I know sharing my story helps because I have been helped by the stories of other courageous souls. I've made mistakes on choosing people to trust and have been betrayed, but I've learned from that, too.

Surrendering daily helps me to recognize God's grace and mercy. It is a gift there for me even when I'm not paying attention. Surrendering isn't about giving up. It's about letting go and letting God direct me. Over the years, I have grown to love Jesus even more. For a long time, I couldn't say that I love Jesus.

Despite the chaos I grew up in, I was taught to believe in a higher power. Now I understand that fearing God means to be in awe of His grace and mercy. Mom told me that because of His suffering, Jesus knows how we feel. He has given me hope so I can navigate the minefield of life and one day I will join Him in heaven.

Faith

Faith has been woven throughout my whole life. I was baptized as a three-month-old baby on December 17, 1950, in my grandparent's Lutheran church. My parents made a vow to teach me all about God the Father, Jesus, and the Holy Spirit.

When I was an adolescent, I attended two years of Saturday confirmation classes to affirm my faith. Even as a young child, I loved standing in our small country church singing at the beginning of each service, "Holy, Holy, Holy, Merciful and Mighty! God in Three Persons blessed Trinity." But I didn't like Sunday school, except when I was four and the teacher gave us graham crackers and orange juice; in sixth grade, I liked having Mom as a wise teacher. Otherwise, I felt self-conscious. The country church where we belonged drew members from the surrounding area. Most of the kids either went to school together or were cousins. Since I went to a different school, I felt like an outsider.

My family was always close, sticking by each other. My sisters and I always looked out for one another. When tragedies occurred, Mom would draw us together and talk about God being with us. Even though I didn't sense God with me, Mom's voice soothed my soul and reassured my mind. I knew she wouldn't lie to me, but when the lights went out at night, I was alone with my anxiety of what tragedy might happen next. I would replay each trauma in my mind. The world was spinning quickly out of control. Alone in the dark, I was filled with unease and began suffering from panic attacks.

On top of our familial tragedies, the nation was in turmoil. The 1960s was a time of great confusion for the country. The national tone of fear trickled all the way down to me, still a young girl who was trying to make sense of the world. It even entered our home on national TV. With each assassination and horrific tales from Vietnam, I questioned if anyone knew what they were doing. No adult seemed to know what they were doing. Why would a loving God do all of this?

Numerous trips were made to the doctor when I was little for recurrent stomach aches, until one day he said, "You worry too much." Well, of course I did! His comment just made me stuff my worries deeper inside me where everything got jumbled up in my head and gut.

In my early thirties, I shamefully caught myself hoping for another tragedy. If someone would die, our family would be brought back to a time of warming togetherness and I would feel secure again. I was desperate for that bond I felt growing up. It seemed in a crisis we were more united, but maybe that was because there were so many of them. My thoughts confused me and gave me horrible guilt. I often wondered what was wrong with me. I felt inept at managing my anger and fear. I didn't want others to see what a mess I had become.

Ironically, my attempts to act tough and ease my pain made me stand out. It didn't help that I had my dad's hot temper. Growing up, he would often yell, "What in the hell is wrong with you? Do you have shit for brains?"

For many years, I believed that I did. Now I would tell my younger self, "Honey, you had way too much coming at you to be able to think clearly. It's okay. We'll find help."

Around 2004, my cousins and I compared notes on our fathers. I discovered that their dad, my uncle, demanded the same question about their brains from them. Grandpa Weets had passed it on to his sons. Dad's brutal words further hindered my ability to deal with confusing emotions. I'm sure he didn't even realize how it affected me. I know that if I were able to tell him today how much it hurt me, he would hug me tight and say he was sorry.

Mom also scolded me growing up. "Don't make a fool of yourself," she admonished. Of course, I often did, feeling inadequate and ashamed. It took many years to see how my beliefs were distorted by fears and skewed by trying to take control of bewildering situations.

Despite believing in God, I didn't have a concept of Him being with me. I didn't fully understand the role of Jesus or the Holy Spirit living inside of me, being my counselor and guide. In childhood, my faith was dependent on my surroundings. I learned about religion from parents, in Sunday school, and by praying with my older sisters.

During my senior year of high school, I confidently announced to my parents, "I've decided that I'm not going to Sunday school anymore."

Dad sternly responded, "The hell you're not!"

His force surprised me, but his care pleased me. It was the first time I realized how important my faith was to him. I finished my class without any further protest.

Before I took my first steps toward recovery, I went to church religiously every Sunday, hoping one day I would figure out what I was missing. I had faith, but I wasn't able to act like it. Despite my spiritual feeling of emptiness, God was there when I needed Him most. I knew something was wrong with me, I just didn't know what. I'd look around at our new home, a new car, a good job, and my husband, and I would think, "Is this all there is to life?" Owen continued to allow me to feel my pain and out of that pain came the greatest gift of my life—a personal relationship with Jesus. There was immense joy, but there were also tsunamis of confusion. I still made attempts to control the uncontrollable, then limping spiritually, I would always come back to surrendering myself to Him.

When I woke the morning of October 4, the day after my realization that I was addicted to alcohol, I had a clear sensation of being cradled like a baby in the arms of my Heavenly Father. What a secure and beautiful feeling! Each time that I share that spiritual experience, I am filled again with the peace, love, and awe I experienced over thirty years ago.

That morning I went with my friend Judy to a meeting filled with people who had made the decision to live sober lives. I watched as she was greeted with smiles and lots of hugs. I wanted that, too! In those gatherings, I heard men and women talk so much about how they prayed; I'd never heard prayer mentioned so much, not even in church. I got to listen to people tell of their brokenness and also how grateful they were to find a path of healing and people to help them.

This awakening led to a period of spiritual growth and strengthening of my relationship with my Lord and Savior Jesus Christ. He was no longer "up there" in Heaven waiting for me, He was living inside me and loving me. But it wasn't an easy road. There were still struggles.

Despite my inexperience, I tried to be a good stepmother and grandmother. Owen still had a lot of guilt about moving an hour away from the kids after his divorce, too. Just six months after my decision to be free of alcohol, I needed to have a fourth back surgery. Insecurity and fear enveloped me as I wondered if Owen would stick by me. My job as a clinic manager was held for me, but after three months I continued to have severe pain and couldn't return to work. The scar tissue and bone chips scraped off my sacral nerve caused unbearable pain.

Once again, I felt like a loser. After having to leave the job I had worked so hard for, my self-esteem plummeted. Losing my ability to function well physically was devastating. I couldn't believe another health crisis was happening.

In a moment of despondency, I said to a family member, "Now I'm not even worth $32,000."

Quickly God said to me, "You are worth more than any dollar amount!"

It was still a miserable situation and it was a long, hard, frustrating road of recovery. As I got through one health problem, another would pop up.

After my spiritual awakening, I had a strong desire to be around women who had a solid Christian faith. I wanted to grow past my crippling immaturity that had held me back and caused friction with others, but I was taught God would reveal more when I was ready. I was told to trust the process and live in today, a concept that had long bewildered me.

I perceived abandonment as a child when Billy died and Mom was in the hospital. I perceived abandonment when floodwaters came and we had to evacuate our house. I perceived abandonment when Tommy died and Dad was hospitalized. Like most teenagers, I was jilted by a man I thought I loved. The beginning of my adult life was ill flavored by these perceived abandonments and the child I was had everything jumbled up inside. It went on and on until God gave me an opportunity to see the world in a different way.

Several years after I realized I was an alcoholic, I met Sister Del Rey. She was the first nun from whom I would seek spiritual direction. My friend Shelia recommended her as a good source to help me grow spiritually. It didn't matter that Sister DelRey was a Catholic nun and I was Lutheran. Our relationship transcended denominations and lived in the realm of spirituality. She was a great source of strength, directness, and love until her death in 2012. Even after her death, I am comforted in remembering her wisdom, love, and compassion.

With Sister DelRey, I grieved all that I went through. She kindly and lovingly sat with me as I sobbed and assured me of the importance of tending to my grief.

With tears staining my cheeks I often asked her, "Where was God when all these cruel life events happened?"

Through her, my eyes were opened to the fact that Jesus had been with me every step. She directed me to a Bible verse from Exodus and she inserted my name, *Delaine, I was with you all along.*

The "Footprints" poem was important to me before sobriety. When I was thirty years old and newly divorced, I transferred from Augustana College in Sioux Falls to the University of South Dakota for a year because my youngest sister Nina lived there with her family. Spending time with her and her kids was wonderful. As Christmas gifts, because I was broke, I painstakingly typed out the poem on an old typewrite using the nicest paper I could afford. I think it accurately explains my faith journey.

Footprints in the Sand

One night I dreamed a dream.
As I was walking along the beach with my Lord.
Across the dark sky flashed scenes from my life.
For each scene, I noticed two sets of footprints in the sand,
One belonging to me and one to my Lord.
After the last scene of my life flashed before me,
I looked back at the footprints in the sand.
I noticed that at many times along the path of my life,
especially at the very lowest and saddest times,
there was only one set of footprints.
This really troubled me, so I asked the Lord about it.
"Lord, you said once I decided to follow you,

You'd walk with me all the way.
But I noticed that during the saddest and
most troublesome times of my life,
there was only one set of footprints.
I don't understand why, when I needed You the most, You
would leave me."
He whispered, "My precious child, I love you and will
never leave you
Never, ever, during your trials and testings.
When you saw only one set of footprints,
It was then that I carried you.

— Anonymous

There is another tongue-in-cheek version that also depicts two long marks in the sand. God said, "That's when I had to drag you."

Accepting the presence of God's grace was a painful process because I couldn't conceive why He let awful things happen, one after another. I was confused and didn't trust Him. There were years of pent up tears I shed like a child as I laid my head in Sister DelRey's lap. I grieved my brother Billy's death and the myriad of other losses. I was previously unable to release my years of sorrow because Mom and I were enmeshed in our pain. How could we not be? When I was drinking, my unhappy emotions were stuffed down by alcohol in a desperate attempt to be rid of them and to feel good.

Today, I can imagine the young child I was, nearly three years old, when Billy died. How I must have repeatedly cried out to Mom, asking for Billy, wanting to know where he was. I imagine Mom holding me as I yelled for him while her own heart was breaking. When she looked at me, she saw him.

For years, Mom was open to my questions about Billy's death She knew I was deeply impacted and she wanted to help me. When Jerri died in 1997, Mom said, "I can't talk about it anymore."

All of Mom's efforts at helping others get help had finally caught up with her. She'd never had time to grieve and didn't go to counseling explaining, "I'm afraid that I would start crying and never stop."

I'm amazed Mom was able to tell me as much about the accident as she did. She taught me to put others first, but eventually my body wore out as hers did.

In the end, I did what she couldn't do. I got help.

Who shall separate us from the love of Christ? Shall trouble or hardship or persecution or famine or nakedness or danger or sword? As it is written, "For your sake we face death all day long; we are considered as sheep to be slaughtered." No, in all things we are more than conquerors through him who loves us. For I am convinced that neither death, nor life, nor angels, nor rulers, nor things present, nor things to come, nor powers, nor height, nor depth, nor anything else in creation, will be able to separate us from the love of God in Christ Jesus our Lord.

(Romans 8:35-39 NIV)

CHAPTER 20
RENEWED FAITH

Over the years, many women who had grown to be my friends and support system moved to other cities evoking familiar feelings of abandonment and depression. I was devastated by each loss. It took prayer, spiritual direction, and counseling to see their departures as a gift from God. It taught me how to heal my deep-seated heartache, how to grieve in healthier ways, and how to have healthy goodbyes.

In recovery, I have better learned the value of relationships. I see how negative experiences help me grow if I chose to learn from them, but it can be painful. Like any couple, Owen and I have gone through rough times. My chronic illnesses and his loss of hearing added stress. It has also brought us closer. In praying together, we find a place of humility. Encouraging each other in our faith has strengthened our bond.

I am striving to be the best version of myself, the person God wanted me to be all along. Surrendering and reminding myself of the Serenity Prayer is key.

God grant me the serenity (peace) to accept the things I cannot change; courage (despite fear) to change the things I can, and wisdom to know the difference.

A friend once told me another version with a touch of humor. *God grant me the serenity to accept the people I cannot change, courage to change the people I can, and wisdom to know that means me!* My ego would like to say I've mastered the lessons of the Serenity Prayer, but that certainly is not true, and it never will be.

Actually, Sister DelRey advised, "Take a *quick* look at yourself and a *long* look at God."

When I falter, it's helpful to be gentle with myself saying, "It's Okay."

When I beat myself, I just get more centered on myself.

After being diagnosed in 1989 with Chronic Fatigue Syndrome, I stumbled upon a copy of *Living with Chronic Illness* by Cheri Register. The following passage has ministered to me often over the years:

"The notion that the Lord totally accepts me where I am at first struck me as a great relief from many of the psychological burdens that chronic illness brings with it: shame about being perfect, guilt about imposing on family and friends, embarrassment at not being able to contain fears and disappointments, humiliation at not being able to overcome physical limitations."

My reality is that I have a number of chronic illnesses that demand attention and lots of rest. They affect what I can do and how much time I can spend with others. When I'm overtired, it's easy for my emotions to become unreliable and for me to become insecure.

It's not always easy to give in to the need to rest; I realize grieving the inability to keep up is normal. At those times, I am gifted with God's helping hand. I am comforted by praying the scripture, "Lord, I believe, help my unbelief." I am my best when I am honest, open, and willing to see where I need help and have the courage to ask for it.

After Sister DelRey's death, I was grateful my friend Patty suggested I get guidance from Sister JoAnn Sturzl. For many years, she taught a spiritual writing class focused on self-exploration. Sister JoAnn has been wonderful in reflecting to me the traits she sees in me, such as love and joy. At the end of our monthly visits, she often asks, "Was this helpful?" My response is always a grateful, "Yes!" I think of regular spiritual direction sessions as having divine oil changes.

A major turning point in my faith was after my fourth back surgery. For a long while when I was bedridden, I did not value myself enough to ask for a pastor to come visit me. I felt we lived too far away and I was always hearing how busy all the pastors were.

Then one day, as I was in bed and unable to do much of anything for myself, I felt a burning desire to take a more active role in my faith. Out of my own spiritual need and my new relationship with Jesus, I wanted to help others. I saw an opportunity to serve by recording Dial-a-Devotion for my church and to find others to volunteer as readers. It was a good way for me to connect with others while laid up. I also wrote Bible quizzes to air on the local Christian TV station.

One day at a very low point of feeling discouraged and depressed, the phone rang. I reluctantly picked it up (there wasn't caller ID) and was surprised that it was the TV station manager calling to ask if I would give my faith testimony on TV. It was close to that time that I heard God whispering my name. In my left ear I clearly heard, "Delaine, Delaine." A week later, a crew from the Christian TV station came to my house to tape my testimony.

When I grew physically stronger, I learned of the new Stephen Ministry training program at my church and I signed up. A Stephen Minister is a lay minister who supplements pastoral care. They are not ordained members of the church, but offer one-on-one confidential care.

After healing enough from my back surgery, I applied and was accepted into the program. During the two-year program, I was diagnosed with another illness and thought I'd have to drop out. Thankfully, the pastor leading the program gave me videos to watch at home and gave me one-on-one sessions for extra training.

Following completion, I served for a brief window as a Stephen Minister to another church member. When I was once again bedridden with pain from my back injury, I had the assurance to seek the help of a Stephen Minister. Love and spiritual guidance was key to my continued spirituality and will to survive. My parents' custom of inviting our local pastors over for a meal and asking for help when needed embedded in me the importance of having a strong relationship with the spiritual guides in our church community.

Owen took the SM course a year after me. What we learned from that program helped our communication skills and gave us encouragement. Having the humility to ask others for help greatly helped our marriage. I arranged for groceries to be picked up, a neighbor boy to mow, asked people from church for help (some brought meals and ate with us), and women in recovery came to the house to have 12 Step meetings.

The next step in my faith journey and education was enrolling in the North American Baptist Seminary[13] to become a family counselor with thoughts of specializing in grief. I was only in my late thirties, but my health was as bad as ever. In one class, I was in too much back pain to sit. Instead of quitting and going home, determination led me to bring some cushions and lie on the floor in the back of the room as I learned.

I went to school part time because I couldn't handle a full load. Each semester, when the credit hour rates would increase,

---

[13] Now the Sioux Falls Seminary.

I would cry and say to Owen, "Why am I even doing this? I may not even be able to work after getting the degree."

Owen lovingly held me and said, "Just think of it as an investment in you. You don't have to do anything with it. You enjoy learning and growing. We'll make it work."

I was officially diagnosed with Chronic Fatigue and Immune Dysfunction Syndrome (CFIDS) in 1990, six months after our granddaughter Hannah was born. Nowadays, when we celebrate her birthday, I think back on how far we have come.

The day after Christmas the year before, I was playing Scrabble with Owen and my mother-in-law Sarah when I noted a weird sensation in my head. I thought it was because I was exhausted and stressed from finishing finals the week before.

When I woke up the next morning, I thought I had a bad case of the flu. I felt too lousy to get up to say goodbye to Sarah, who was taking a flight home that morning. Concerned about getting her sick, I called out, "Goodbye, I love you," from the bedroom.

At 4 a.m. the next morning, I awoke so dizzy I could barely turn my head.

I couldn't believe how much energy it took to move over to wake Owen and say, "I need to go the emergency room."

He was up in a flash.

"And I need help dressing," I moaned.

"Where are you?" he asked.

I was lying on the floor, too dizzy to stand.

In the emergency room, I was given saline intravenously; automatic blood pressure readings would startle and make me feel like I was jumping out of my skin. I kept grabbing at the cuff to make it stop, irritating the nurse. Eventually, I was given the diagnosis of the flu and sent home feeling scared and like an idiot.

After six weeks, my "flu" symptoms only got worse. I had to grasp Owen's arm tightly to walk to the car and then into the clinic. I had lost weight so the doctor caring for me decided I should go to the hospital for tests. He agreed I had something more than the flu.

I had lost 13 pounds for no apparent reason and my vision was blurred almost all the time. Dizziness was a constant. In addition, I suffered bouts of nausea, sore throats, profuse sweating, shortness of breath, and abject fatigue. I wasn't just tired. The fatigue was so bad that at times turning over in bed was hard to do. I couldn't even bathe myself. There were days it was even difficult to talk, forcing me to communicate by writing notes. It was always comical when the person I was conversing with started writing a response.

I chuckled, shook my head and wrote, "You can talk."

Owen would sometimes have to help me to and from the bathroom. When I couldn't take being confined to the bedroom any longer, I resorted to crawling on my hands and knees to the living room. It proved too much at times and my heart would race. My body being so out of whack caused me to have anxiety and panic attacks. I was overly sensitive to lights and sounds. Here I was, only forty years old and not able to take care of myself. It was utterly humiliating. To make it worse, we didn't know what was going on in my body.

I called a dear friend and cried, "I get so sick trying to get to meetings. I'm scared. I can't even be a good wife."

It was the right call to make. She served as a role model, guiding me to living a healthier life emotionally and spiritually, along with keeping a great sense of humor. She told me to lean on God and not worry about missing meetings. She reminded me that I was important to Owen and that I was still valuable and had a lot to offer our marriage by just being me. Those words would carry me through many doubts.

When diagnosed, I didn't know of anyone else with CFIDS. It was lonely not having any resources, computers weren't normal home fixtures to look up information or find support groups. Through my network of friends, I was eventually introduced to a female physician who had to quit her dermatology practice because of the illness. She was a lifeline for me and I found comfort when she shared encouraging scriptures with me.

Although I felt miserable on the inside, I somehow looked fine on the outside. It was a blessing and a curse.

When my Dad saw me in the hospital bed he said, "You look good. I expected to see you looking sick."

I felt discounted when people would say "Chronic fatigue? Well sure, I'm tired all the time, too."

Little did they understand the havoc the disease created in my life and in my marriage. There were times Owen received uninformed and judgmental advice that I was just looking for attention. CFIDS is something that can't be cured with an afternoon nap. Whenever I woke up, I felt exhausted and unrefreshed.

In tears, I went to Pastor Julie to tell her my diagnosis. It was such a blessing the way she not only listened to me but also believed me.

Her response, "Oh, I was afraid of that," truly spoke to my heart.

She told me she almost cried because she knew how hard it was to be a pioneer since she was the first female pastor in our church. Her understanding was a godsend.

Pastor Julie validated all my symptoms and feelings. We even laughed together about how well I looked. There were times I wished I looked sick so that people would understand. I was hoping for people to understand something I didn't even really understand myself.

It was during the onset of CFIDS, when I was attending the Seminary, that my mother said, "Honey, I believe that God gave you your recovery program to help you deal with this illness."

Even though she didn't understand the path I was working to live a better life, she saw the positive results and how it helped me to be stronger in my faith. Her empathy was one of the greatest gifts she ever gave me, as well as her daily phone calls for the long six weeks before I received my diagnosis.

The unexpectedness of CFIDS would often catch me off guard. I might feel well enough to start a meal or wash the dishes, but often crash in my effort, needing to lie down. My energy well ran very shallow. It was baffling to us how one minute I was well enough to do a task and the next minute was physically unable. I could get ready to go somewhere and get out to the car, but then have to have Owen help me back in the house.

Feelings of depression and anxiety accompanied the fatigue. We didn't have the Internet to look up information on the disease and few doctors knew about it. My oldest sister Jerri, who lived in Charlotte, North Carolina, read of a doctor who was doing research that held some promises for a cure. Out of love and concern, she went to the doctor's clinic on the other side of the city to get information she then mailed to me. Years later, I returned the favor by sending her information about her ovarian cancer diagnosis.

The first six years I had CFIDS were the roughest. Since then, the symptoms have waxed and waned. My worst level of fatigue is accompanied by depression and feelings of loneliness. These emotions are miserable, but they serve as cues to get even more rest than usual. The body and mind are pressed down, limited in what they can do.

After she learned of my illness from a mutual friend, Kay Langin sent me a get-well card and a letter. She was also in recovery and happened to be going through a divorce. We started exchanging letters regularly. We have been penpals for twenty-five years, sharing our deepest fears and highest joys. Her friendship and letters made me feel less alone even though we were direct opposites. She referred to me as the City Mouse and herself as Country Mouse. The letters I wrote to her helped me process what I was feeling. Many of the weekly letters we exchanged had funny stories of goofs we'd made. A good laugh lightened my heart.

During this time, I was still attempting to attend classes at the North American Baptist Seminary. After my diagnosis, I gained some strength and tried to return to class, but I got terribly dizzy and fatigued. I tried to steam roll my way back to health in a desperate attempt to finish school.

A turning point came when my Stephen Minister, Connie Salmela, asked, "Do you have to take a class right now?"

Of course, I did! I needed to finish. I had a determination and persistence that was beyond good sense. Connie's question rolled around in me for days, along with the wretched fatigue and dizziness. In the end, it was her question that enabled me to let go and surrender. After completing about half of the required credits, I made the tough decision to quit, thinking one day I would return. Instead, my condition worsened and surviving each day was a challenge.

Dad had shown me a newspaper clipping early on that said, "You won't die from this illness, but you'll wish you would."

Many times, I thought about ending my life. I tried to devise a way that it would appear an accident and not suicide.

One-day Owen came home from lunch and surprised me when he said, "I never know if I'm going to walk in and find you hanging somewhere."

It was at that point that I promised him I would never take my life. Despite my promise, the desire to die still sometimes came over me.

After taking a step back and seeing all that I had accomplished, I realized achieving the master's degree in counseling wasn't the gift God had in mind for me. Achieving a better understanding of myself was the true goal. I grew more confident in prayer and discovered how to apply faith to everyday life.

I love to learn and grow. I have pursued educational opportunities with the goal of bettering my understanding of the world around me and myself. Most of all, it was to best nurture the gift of faith that God has given me.

For several years, I listened to Bible teacher Joyce Meyer's teaching tapes. I was grasping onto life in any way I could. Looking to God was the focus I needed. God put a joy in my heart that was beyond my ability. There were times I could answer the "How are you?" question from friends and family with, "My body is the pits, but I have joy in my heart."

The wretched fatigue prevented me from exercising and keeping my muscles strong. My pelvic floor muscles grew even weaker from my immobility, to the point of severe spasms preventing me from walking and sitting. Owen wisely described the spasms as Charlie horses. Although he didn't feel my pain, he could describe what I couldn't. I was surprised and touched by the depths of his understanding and the way he tried to relate.

Owen and I spent thousands of dollars on alternative treatments when all the western medicine methods had been exhausted. Regular reflexology treatments accompanied by lymph node massages seemed to make a big difference. Breathing exercises helped get oxygen to my hungry cells and muscles. A diet of increased salt also made a difference.

Therapy sessions helped me deal with the anger and depression. The guidance of Sister DelRey and Pastor Julie aided me in facing my grief and led me to a deeper relationship with God. Wonderful friends helped me know I was loved and not forgotten. Weekly, three friends also in recovery met with me at my house for mutual support. We embraced the feeling of community by sharing our lives with each other, with both tears and laughter.

Laughter gave me needed reprieves. Recently, I read in the magazine *Church Health*: "Laughter and rejoicing need to be part of our faith life. Think of something funny that has happened and thank God for giving us humor in our lives."

Of course, the love of my husband sustained me throughout it all. For a number of years, I was barely able to leave the house. Owen occasionally helped me with baths and dried my hair.

He even helped me with a bedpan for a time and would joke, "Now I'm in charge of how much toilet paper you use."

His ability to joke during these tense times lightened the mood. It played a large role in me falling in love with him. I adore his laugh, his smile, and his prayers for me in the middle of the night when I am afraid I'll never get well.

On one of my worst days, Owen held me on his lap and asked me, "Will you marry me?"

His proposal was his way of telling me that he would always be there for me no matter what. He was recommitting himself to me and us as a couple.

Love didn't make the illness go away, but it made it bearable.

As I got stronger, I received further encouragement. In a wheelchair, I traveled by air to Rapid City to attend a mother-daughter luncheon with my stepdaughter, Sylvia and her two daughters, Sarah and Sunny. Sitting with Sylvia at a Burger King while the girls played, she told me of Sunny's unspoken prayer at school. Each day her teacher asked if there were any prayer requests from the class. When asked if there were any unspoken requests Sunny would raise her hand. After this went on awhile, the concerned teacher approached Sylvia who then asked Sunny what was wrong.

Sunny shyly muttered, "I just want my Grandma to get better."

Hearing that gave me a resolve like nothing else. I was going to do whatever it took to make that little girl's prayer come true. To this day, recalling that story of pure innocent compassion feeds my soul.

CFIDS has simultaneously tested and strengthened my faith, as have all my maladies. I continue to suffer from the disease but it's more manageable now. Sometimes it still prevents me from attending family or social events because I lack the energy.

I know God was at work in me during the darkest times. He didn't heal me as I prayed, but He brought me through. The suffering also prepared me for the health crises to come.

As I got stronger, Mom suggested I do what Sister DelRey did as a Spiritual Director. Sister DelRey would describe it as "listening a person to life," emphasizing the value of a person being heard. I told Mom I could *never* do what Sister DelRey did, but it sparked a light in me.

So, the next step in my faith journey was taking a spiritual direction program centered in Yankton, SD, 90 miles from home. Thankfully, the classes were mostly online with a few residencies a year in Yankton during the two-year program. I wanted to do it!

I got the three references needed and did a phone interview with the head of the program at the Sacred Heart Monastery's Benedictine Peace Center. The nun who led the program told me she believed my health would be a negative factor. Because of that, they wanted to give the opening to someone who was sure they could finish. Well, I knew I could!

"If you put a recliner in the classroom I know that I can do it," I boldly told her.

I didn't get a quick yes, but it was a yes. The next hurdle was getting someone to drive me for the residencies in May and September. Sister DelRey suggested someone for me to ask. I was delighted to share the trip with three women in their late thirties; I was forty-five. Christina O'Hara gladly took on the chauffer role driving my van, so I could lie down in the front passenger seat.

The goal of the spiritual direction program was for each of us to grow spiritually by getting in touch with our vulnerabilities, brokenness, and faith. This would prepare us to serve God by listening to other's sacred stories.

When the program was completed, a student was certified to be a companion or guide with whom others could share their experiences of God. The program did not produce counselors, instead created faithful individuals with developed listening skills.

It was a time for me to grow closer to God. It was truly a formative experience for my faith, sparked by the desire God put in me as told in Philippians 2:1, "for it is God who works in you to will and act in order to fulfill his good purpose." It was an honor to be joined with men and women of deep faith and far more experience.

When I got accepted into the program, Owen and I made a visit to Mom to tell her.

I was sure she'd be excited, but instead she said, "Now don't think that you're going to change me!"

Then Owen said, "She's going to become a nun!"

In response, I had a deeply spiritual moment where I wanted to choke them both!

In September of 2006, I began that spiritual journey. I was sure it was going to be this wonderful, holy journey. When I went to the first intensive training at the monastery, one of the instructors showed me the classroom. I wept when I saw the lone recliner waiting for me. While I was grateful, it was humbling. I knew that once again it wasn't going to be easy to be different; there was no covering up my vulnerability.

Then, all hell broke loose. A stipulation of the class was that we were not to miss any of the three-day residencies at the monastery unless there was a death. Halfway through the second residency, a daughter-in-law had surgery for breast cancer. When it turned out to be stage three, worse than we expected, I told the instructor I had to leave even though I knew I might be expelled. Amidst many tears, I was met with great compassion and assurance that I would get an opportunity to make up the missed classes.

After our last class at 10:00 p.m. that evening, Christina and another friend drove me home. Owen and I were relieved to be together. Early the next morning we traveled across the state to be with our son, daughter-in-law, and their children.

During the next two years a lot happened. In addition to our daughter-in-law battling breast cancer, my mom died half way through the SD program and I grieved her death. Escaping an unsafe situation, several family members moved in with us for almost a year. While it was stressful, I can't imagine the stress they were under. We got a new puppy. My sisters and brother-in-law came from out of town came and spent many weekends at our house. I got strep throat, pneumonia, and the doctor found a suspicious spot on my lung which caused us immense worry, but over a few years it shrank.

Despite it all, God carried me through and helped me grow. After finishing the program, I used my new skills listening to seekers who wanted someone to listen to their story and help them see where God was at work in their lives. I was soon to see how what I learned in the two-year program would help me continue to grow deeper in my faith.

In 2013, I was diagnosed with viral meningitis and began the process of letting go of ministry work at church, as well as mentoring women in recovery. My work was important to me and made up a large part of my identity, but I knew that my worsening health wouldn't allow me to go on.

My sickness stopped my ability to read during church services, to serve communion alongside my husband, and to teach Bible studies. Following this turbulent time, I also suffered from a cornea surgery, a car accident, and went through intense testing to be diagnosed with Postural Orthostatic Tachycardia Syndrome (POTS), another illness very few people have heard of.

POTS is when a person has an excessive heart rate and a drop in blood pressure, especially when getting out of bed or from a lying position. When I asked the neurologist how to explain it to others, he said to tell them that the wiring to my heart is screwed up.

Overall blood volume or blood pooling in the abdomen or legs can lead to a rapid heartbeat, fatigue, heat intolerance, difficulty exercising, nausea, lightheadedness, shortness of breath, and trouble sleeping. Standing is difficult. I've experienced all the symptoms, as well as the anxiety caused by my blood pressure and pulse. It can take a person with POTS ten times more energy just to stand than it does for someone without it.

When I was diagnosed with CFIDS in 1989, it was much harder to find information and support groups than it is now. The Internet is not only filled with information but connects individuals. Of course, nothing replaces a relationship with a physician.

I was grateful that I had Sister JoAnn to talk to about the havoc this caused in my life.

During one visit I declared, "Sometimes I just have to be hit in the head by a two-by-four to get things!"

With a chuckle she responded, "You have been!"

Laughing along with her, I pondered how now more than ever I understood God was with me. I'd like to say that I never again doubted His love or presence in times of need. My encouragement comes from scripture in the book of Romans 8:35-39 that tells me that nothing, not sickness nor pain, will separate me from God's love.

Taking a step back from all I'd lost and looking at my situation, I knew I had to allow myself to grieve and I had to once again make choices that lined up with my abilities and limitations. I had just celebrated twenty-five years of recovery and felt called to share my story with the teenage group at church. I thought it was important to tell them that, at the age of sixteen, I lost my virginity, when I was drunk, to a guy I was sure I loved. I equated sex with love, but later found out that he did not love me. In the end, I found addiction ministry and it has been my passion ever since.

God has given me the strength to share my story so that others can take comfort in it and learn from it. I firmly believe that it was God who put that desire in me. When the opportunity presented itself at my church, Our Savior's Lutheran, to plan an event about faith and addiction, I enthusiastically offered my services.

For over five years, I have had the privilege of arranging speakers to share their faith stories with our congregation and visitors. Guest speakers have told how they broke free from their alcohol or other drug addictions. I arranged for addiction specialists to be brought in for all ages. Recovery agencies were also invited to bring helpful information about the disease and how and where to get help.

My fervent prayer that God would bless this endeavor was answered. My dream that something similar would spread to other churches in the area came to fruition. Using our church's program as an example, the Synod Associate Pastor spearheaded forming the group, Communities Facing Addiction.

So far, nine churches in the Sioux Falls area are taking part in addiction ministry. We are all working ardently to change the beliefs and stigmas of addiction among our fellow believers. As brothers and sisters of Christ, we are tasked with helping each other. I have seen God's hand in it from the beginning. I am so privileged to serve Him and pray that He is glorified in this ministry.

Shortly after the addiction ministry began at my church, I talked with Sister DelRey about my part in leading the ministry.

She asked me, "Do you realize how big this is?"

I don't think I did.

I was in awe when she said, "You were made for this moment."

I know it was God who put the desire in me and led me on this path.

God has turned my sorrows and sins into a healing voice. I share my story so that others will know they are not alone. I pray to God for His grace to help me live out this journey faithfully. He has taken my past and made me more compassionate and understanding of others and myself. It was hard walking through all the pain, but how I rejoice that God provides.

God's love and healing touch has transformed my past self, giving me joyous freedom today.

"When we share our stories, it opens up our hearts for other people to share their stories. And it gives us the sense that we are not alone on this journey."

— Janine Shepherd

CHAPTER 21
GOD'S TIMING TO TELL THE STORY

2004

Many years ago, I made a silent vow that I would never speak in public about Billy's death. I knew it would hurt Dad too much to tell others about how he accidently backed over and killed my brother. It pained me to even think about it. The subject made anyone hearing about it wince. While we didn't discuss the accident as a family, but we still told funny stories about Billy. Some families have a rule never to speak a deceased loved one's name, but it was important for us to remember him.

Each year on May 12, Billy's birthday, I called Mom and Dad. We never talked long, but it was nice to acknowledge his day. I thought that maybe someday, after Dad passed away, I might find the courage to tell the story. I talked about it with Mom many times, in counseling sessions, and multiple codependency treatments over the years. Along the way, I learned that by examining the painful memories, I found clarity and healing to equip me in helping others and for serving God.

There is a saying that a coincidence is God choosing to remain anonymous. It was no coincidence that one week after Dad died in September of 2004, I was asked to give a Temple Talk, a personal testimony in front of the congregation.

I was a co-leader of the prayer ministry team during our church's book study on *A Purpose Driven Life* by Rick Warren. My dear friend, Connie Salmela, was the leader of all the teams. She knew my story and one night after a meeting asked me to share parts of it with our faith community.

My first response was, "I can't handle giving a talk at all five services. I don't have enough energy."

She quickly replied, "All you have to do is one."

I very much trusted her opinion and said, "Okay, I will do it."

The next day, I called our senior pastor to let him know I had been asked and to find out the amount of time I would have for my talk.

He first responded, "Well, we have a really busy schedule this Sunday."

Breathing a sigh of relief, I said, "Then it's probably better not to add one more thing."

"Oh no, I didn't mean that, but you'll have exactly three minutes and you must keep it at that," he quickly said.

I knew that since the service was being televised, respecting the time limit was vital.

God's Timing to Tell the Story

My faith story in three minutes. . .wow. Billy's accident flashed through my mind. Dad had just died, and I thought, *No, this is too soon.*

In the following days I worked diligently on my testimony. Through the process I continually thanked God for the opportunity and asked for His strength to empower me to share my story. I prayed often that the Holy Spirit would give me the precise words to convey my love and faith in Him.

The Sunday I was scheduled to speak quickly arrived. Sitting next to my husband, I prayed. The idea of sharing Billy's accident with the congregation still gnawed at me. I continued to pray as I walked to the pulpit, "Okay God, then You give me the words."

A friend later told me that I had looked calm, but I was shaking with nerves as I laid down my notes. I was grateful for the opportunity and the privilege to share my story. However, opening up about something that had haunted me for decades was a bit daunting. Here is my testimony of October 2005:

As a child, I was taught about God, that Jesus came to die for my sins, and that someday, through believing in Him, I would go to heaven.

As a child, some tragic deaths happened in our family; one of them being when my dad accidently backed over my brother. Even though I attended Sunday School and church, I felt scared and ashamed a lot of the time. I wondered if those tragedies really were God's will and wondered why

He would do that to us. I thought our family must have done something to deserve it.

As an adult, there were more losses and I made some wrong choices when trying to deal with them. The harder I tried to come up with solutions, the more frustrating my life became. My mom assured me many times that God wasn't causing bad things. I could understand that in my head but not in my heart.

Then eighteen years ago, at a low point in my life, I shared with some friends the loneliness and fear I was feeling. On the outside I looked okay. I had a good paying job, a new house, and a wonderful husband, yet I felt empty.

Through their help, I came to understand that God was constantly reaching out to me to try to help me through these situations. I learned that I needed to surrender to Him and keep my focus on Him to help me, instead of always trying to come up with my own solutions that just weren't working.

I embraced God's reaching out to me and began the process of realizing God's purpose in my life and that He would take away all my pain, my weaknesses, and my incompleteness and use it to help others to glorify Him.

That loneliness and constant fear is gone. I am grateful for the gift of faith He has given me through hearing His Word, the privilege of serving Him, and having Him continually reveal His purposes for my life.

Yes, I still have difficulties. My dad just died and my mother hasn't been well. I have some health challenges and our son is in Iraq. I'm not saying that for you to feel sorry for *me, but to tell you that God is greater than all of that and while I am weak, He is strong, and I don't have to do it on my own anymore.*

Before church that Sunday, I called Mom to let her know I was giving a brief talk, so she could watch the televised church service. Later, I asked her how she felt about me sharing Billy's death with the congregation and the TV audience. Relieved, she told me she was grateful. Finally, she felt heard.

It was as if a weight was lifted from both of our shoulders. My brief talk was healing for both of us. If she was alive today, I am sure she would be proud and grateful that in these pages I have shared with you some of the good and the bad our family has experienced.

"The resurrection of Jesus will let you retrieve your own past, so that you can remember with truth, not self-deception; so that you can accept yourself with thanksgiving, not despair; so that you can confess what is necessary to confess, not hide behind the fig leaf of blaming others, so that you can retrieve God's justification of your life with faith, not strive to justify your life with your own accomplishments."

— from *What Shall I Say?* by Walter R. Bousman & Susan M. Setzer

CONCLUSION

It was an awakening when Evelyn Leite, a codependency counselor said, "You don't trust anyone."

I was affronted and argued that I did. When she asked me who, I said that I trusted her.

"That doesn't count," she replied.

"Why not?" I challenged.

"Because you pay me," was her reply.

Her honesty triggered my stubbornness and I was resolute that I would start trusting. Easier said than done, but since then I have done a lot of work on myself. In the last thirty-one years, I have gradually expanded my trust as I meet with others and we expose broken parts of ourselves. I learned that the one I distrusted the most was me. I have, on occasion, been stung by my openness, but I have grown because of those hurts and it was worth the risk.

Over fifteen years ago, God gave me the desire to join a group of women writers at my church. I wrote about my life in bits and pieces both hard and hilarious. Taking the steps of faith to put in writing some unflattering parts of myself to share with others has included lots of checking my motivation, tears, prayers, and help from others. It did not come easily. Over the years, I have been able to share deeper parts of myself. Sister DelRey taught me that each time I tell my story, I experience more clarity and healing.

Over the years and through the chapters of this book, I have learned a great deal. I saw my parents with a new vision as I realized how much they strove to overcome adversities to keep our family together and moving forward. Through a comment from my cousin, Joy, I saw my parents in a new light and have been amazed at their love for each other.

No matter what we go through, it is important to both share with others and lend a listening ear. The innumerable groups and individuals I have leaned on made a huge impact on my life. Enduring would not have been possible without them. I believe being heard is a fundamental need for each person.

Even though my parents did the best they could, childhood left me with many wounds that I later used alcohol to mask and did not properly treat until adulthood. For many years, I lived with survivor's guilt and the weight of my parents' sorrow. I didn't realize I was trying to take on their pain. It took much soul searching to realize that no one was to blame.

It wasn't my Dad's fault for the unfortunate accident that killed Billy. It wasn't Kenny's fault he moved away and we lost touch. It wasn't my grandparents' fault that Tommy's car wasn't equipped with a seat belt when he was hit by the drunk driver.

Conclusion

It wasn't my fault that Jerri died of ovarian cancer and I escaped it. The deaths, fires, and floods were not my family's punishment from God, but merely the cruelties of life.

In *My Grandfather's Blessings*, Rachel Remen writes, "Grieving may be one of the most fundamental of life skills. It is the way the heart can heal from loss and go on to love again and grow wise. If it were up to me, it would be taught in kindergarten, right up there with taking turns and sharing."[14]

I have learned that though I cannot forget my past, I must not live in it. By delving further into my history and embracing my grief, God has given me further healing and growth. I trust that there is more to come. I am relieved parents and children nowadays have support groups and other avenues to talk with safe people about their feelings. I hope that it gives them help in dealing with their painful feelings.

A wise woman once told me that even if we don't acknowledge our grief, our body feels it. Perhaps since I couldn't mourn the losses of my life in a healthy manner, my immune system was weakened. Health problems have followed me every step of the way.

In the end, the answer is finding hope in God. By trusting Him as my guide, the path through life is a good one. Faith did not come to me overnight. It is something I have both worked at and surrendered to, but to be clear, it is not what I have done, it is what God has done. It is about how He has redeemed my past and given me hope for the future.

---

[14] www.rachelremen.com/books/my-grandfathers-blessings

In his sixties, Grandpa Joe told me he had lived a good life. For many years, I didn't understand how he could say that after enduring so much hardship including the death of three children at young ages. Despite everything I have been through, I can also say that I have lived a wonderful life. God has carried me through.

He has blessed me with a loving family and a joy to live life. To help us endure the unbearable, God gave us a sense of humor and we so enjoy laughing!

EPILOGUE
GATHERING PIECES

As I was striving to finish this collection of memories I felt overwhelmed, stressed, and discombobulated when something my spiritual director Sister DelRey had said popped to mind that helped me. Several weeks after Sister DelRey returned from a trip to Uganda, I asked how she was doing.

Her response was, "I'm still gathering pieces."

As I recalled her statement I knew what I needed to do. So, I jotted down events that had occurred in just the last four months.

Last November, I took Owen to the ER for what turned out to be indigestion rather than a heart attack—he had one twenty years ago, so we couldn't ignore the symptoms. The following morning, he fell backwards off the front step of our house while doing some exercises without the benefit of a railing. That evening, I was feeling stressed as I shared some of my faith story with my church's confirmation kids and their parents. I felt like I failed and fulfilled a childhood admonition from Mom, "Don't make a fool of yourself." The next morning, I cancelled my dental appointment to get a crown so I could take Owen to an orthopedic doctor. We lucked out when x-rays showed no fracture.

My December time line included: a fun overnight visit from one of Owen's younger sisters; Owen's broken hearing aids and trips to the VA Audiology; our oldest son here overnight along with our adult granddaughter; a two-hour dental appointment for a crown; a follow-up appointment for Owen at North Central Heart; my two cataract surgeries, and a 2:30 a.m. ER visit for Owen again for chest pain, This time he was kept overnight for extensive tests; once again we were grateful for good reports.

The quieter January I expected didn't happen. I hurt my tailbone tripping over a cord and that entailed (pun intended) daily chiropractor treatments for two weeks; trouble again with Owen's hearing aids and another trip to the VA; a long overdue reunion with my dorm roommate from X-ray school; a bone marrow biopsy that didn't give clear answers to my chronic anemia and low white count; not one but both cars with dead batteries on the same day; an MRCP of my pancreas in follow-up to last December's hospitalization; Owen was diagnosed with Influenza A.

During February, we had lots of kids home to help us and for them to go ice fishing; overnighters for nine nights. Owen's sister and her husband from Rapid City surprised us with an afternoon visit. We met our grandson Stephen's girlfriend from Montana when she and Stephen's half-brother from Wyoming paid us a morning visit on their way to attend Stephen's Army

Gathering Pieces

Boot Camp graduation ceremony. Adult granddaughter Sunny was a welcome frequent overnight guest. We began using Home Health care services. Son John went with us for Owen's evaluation at the VA Hospital Occupational Therapy department. His entertaining comments made an interesting session.

I also gathered pieces of many joys I had: attending The Nutcracker with two granddaughters, a quiet Christmas with just the two of us, exciting football games, holding hands with Owen as we watched romance movies as he recuperated, wonderful friends stopping over, watching our church service on TV, and serving each other communion using the beautiful earthenware chalice I found at a rummage sale last year for ten cents. We invited old friends for a visit and we had an uplifting visit with a pastor from our church. My Stephen Minister Janiece and friends brought food and support.

Then I mailed my memoirs to the editor in preparation for publishing. It was hard letting go.

As I listed these pieces, I felt a peace. It has been a healing process to take time to look back and gather my thoughts, remove the clutter, and digest all that God has brought me through. There was a time when so much happening would have triggered the PTSD of childhood traumas, but it was the **gathering of the pieces and telling others** that enabled me to eventually "walk in peace and not in pieces."

ABOUT THE AUTHOR

Delaine grew up in Trent, population 200 counting cats and dogs. She has two sisters in Sioux Falls and a sister and brother in heaven. She currently lives in Sioux Falls, SD with her husband Owen and their cockapoo Sophie. She loves being Grandma Dee to nineteen grand-children and great-grandma to two little ones. She is a graduate of Augustana University, a spiritual director and addiction ministry advocate. Being creative and helping others are a few of her passions, inspiring her to write this memoir of hope and healing.

APPENDIX
SERENITY PRAYER

— REINHOLD NIEBUHR (1892-1971)

*God grant me the serenity
to accept the things I cannot change;
courage to change the things I can;
and wisdom to know the difference.
Living one day at a time;
enjoying one moment at a time;
accepting hardships as the pathway to peace;
taking, as He did, this sinful world
as it is, not as I would have it;
trusting that He will make all things right
if I surrender to His Will;
that I may be reasonably happy in this life
and supremely happy with Him
forever in the next.
Amen.*[15]

---

[15] Read more at http://www.beliefnet.com/prayers/protestant/addiction/serenity-prayer.aspx#S72sJ6l4dstusx6c.99

CPSIA information can be obtained
at www.ICGtesting.com
Printed in the USA
FFHW022103141118
49388517-53733FF